THE STREET GOD

"I WON WITHOUT TELLING"

Christian Hayward

The Street God Entertainment

Cleveland, OH

PRINTED IN THE UNITED STATES OF AMERICA

First edition published 2015

For information regarding discounts for bulk purchases, please contact The Street God Entertainment at info@thestreetgod.com.

ISBN 978-0-9964967-0-4 (pbk)

I dedicate this book ...

First of all, I'd like to acknowledge the fact that I'm nothing without God and that I'm thankful for being rescued.

I dedicate this book to my grandmother and every single mom who stayed to accept the task of raising what you created, despite all short comings.

Uncle Tuggie for being my navigation system during my journey in the jungle and my Aunt Val for always rolling with me, right or wrong.

My friend/brother E-Bay for saying, "Chris, write a book." No matter how many times I laughed, he kept saying it and pushing me.

I thank Kim for always believing in me when I didn't believe in myself. And to my friend Cookie, who was with me when I picked up the pen and began to write The Street God, thanks for the encouragement.

A special shout out to all the fallen soldiers, R.I.P. Lil Boo, Wahgy, Man (Orlando), E.B, Boo (Prince), Bubba, Lil B (Dickens), and O.G. Greyhound.

Lastly, I thank East 93rd for building and molding me.

To all my solid brothers, we've made the street hustle a never ending war against our own instead of a stepping stone to uplift each other into better positions in the world that's built for us to lose (Genocide).

I'll always love and respect the street hustle, but as long as you continue to play nothing you have is truly yours. We are recklessly killing our own for territory and money that's not ours.

REMEMBER…*A Snitch Anywhere is a Threat to Every Hustler in the World.*

Sincerely,

Christian

Introduction

Some may not agree that Michael Jordan was the best ever. It's all a matter of opinion. But I'm sure we all agree that he played the game by the rules, he was full of passion and he gave it all he had every second that he was on the court.

When I stepped off the porch at thirteen years old my uncle told me to be the best at whatever I did. It didn't matter if I was dealing, robbing, stealing, or killing, I was to be the best and I was to make sure my heart was connected, or I wouldn't last. I never understood why my uncle took time out to babble these things to a small boy who didn't see any harm in making a few dollars. Besides, he was a dope fiend. What did he know?

Regardless of what my uncle told me, a lot of things inspired this book. The streets, spending time in jail, hard times, and travelling, But most of all, it was the major players like Big Meech and others like him who were never able to tell their story. It was the Jay Z's and 50 Cents of the world who made the streets their own power channel to transition from the streets to where they are today.

On June 16, 2014 at LIV Nightclub in Miami, I saw Floyd Mayweather, Jr. spend what seemed like a million dollars on bottles of the best that money could buy while he took photos with everyone, and I can't lie, I was impressed. But more than anything, I was inspired! I saw that a guy my height, my age and my stature could be set for life because of the same efforts of the greats I've just mentioned. When I left the club, I saw Mayweather in the lobby, I looked him in his eyes and said, "I love you Floyd." I didn't feel like a homosexual or anything. I meant it.

The next morning when I woke up two images played in my mind. The sight of standing next to the man who carried every dope boy's dream (a million dollars) in a bag, for recreation, and also my uncle sitting in front of me when he told me, "the best hustler is the man who sales himself." That was the moment that I realized that I had been risking my life for pennies for over twenty years, and I picked up a pen and began to write.

On December 22, 2006 I was released from the penitentiary for the second time. All I could think about was how each and every time I got out, my granny looked older. This time, I had been gone for 7 ½ years. The world was different. All I had was my 170 pound, 5' 9" frame, no money and without a plan. This time I felt different about the world. I had a better understanding about my health, about people and the importance of being financially stable. I knew I had to be mentally and physically conditioned at all times to stay ahead. Most importantly, I was confident that I would excel. No doubt, I would hustle. Real street niggas never think they're going to get caught. They only see the gold at the tunnels end.

My cousin Janice picked me up. I was nervous, anxious and ready, all at once. We went to Richmond Mall. The first person I saw was Ob, a guy I met in jail several years back from 141st and St. Clair. He was released a year before I was. I was happy to run into him at the mall. After we talked, he gave me $300 and some great advice. I remember thinking, "what the fuck am I gonna do with this?" but as the days passed, I appreciated that $300 more and more.

Next, I visited my granny, the love of my life. We laughed and had great talks. But she was sick, which is what she told me two weeks before I was released but I still acted as if I didn't know. Before I left her house she said, "Chris, I don't want you to get killed." I promised her I wouldn't, but what she didn't know was that I was playing for keeps and nobody was eligible for mercy. I made her that promise with confidence.

I was still young and ruthless, hungrier than ever. I just had to watch and learn because the streets changed every second. When I left to go to prison that last time all me and my boys worried about was vice, (unmarked cars). And if you were weak you worried about the jack boys, but there was no such thing as snitching. Back then the streets were fun. The goons had brains. I still believed in the game wholeheartedly. I had the passion to play and the ability to continue. I also still lived by my code and morals. In fact, I was blinded by my old memories of the 1990s crack game. I didn't know the ratio to win had switched and that fake was the new real. But I would soon find out.

Up The Way

Section One (THE "HOOD")

- Gibson
- Benham
- Anderson
- Orleans
- Aetna

Section Two (Across Union to the right, but also a part of East 93rd)

- Raymond
- Laisy
- Marah
- Bessemer
- Fuller
- Easton

Section Three (located further to the right, past Kinsman)

- Dickens
- Manor

- Mt. Auburn

- Sophia

- East 102nd

Section Four (left of Aetna Road)

- Dunlap

- Sandusky

- Prince

- Reno

- Way

- Nelson

Section Five

- Gaylord

- Pratt

1

I can only start at what I can remember. In 1982, my house was full. Our address, 9404 Gibson was the first and only address I had ever known. My granny, aunt, uncle and his pregnant girlfriend. Sometimes my other uncle lived there with us, as well, in our little three bedroom house.

My grandfather Jimmy (not biological), was the only person I ever knew as a father figure. He came over on the weekends. I thought my life was normal. No father or mother but still for some reason I felt secure. Back then, our neighborhood was terrible but when you're five years old, as long as you had people to play with you were cool.

Gibson, the street where I lived was located off east 93rd two streets over from Union, which was the main intersection. Neighboring streets are Benham, Anderson, Orleans, and Aetna. This was considered our "Hood" or Section One. Everyone in the East 93rd to 103rd radius was "family", anybody else were simply allies.

Across Union to the right, you had Section Two, also a part of East 93rd. This section included Raymond, Laisy, Marah, Bessemer, Fuller and Easton. Located further to the right, past Kinsman was Dickens, Manor, Mt. Auburn, Sophia and East 102nd or Section Three. To the left of Aetna was Dunlap, Sandusky, Prince, Reno, Way, and Nelson, or Section Four. Section Five included those living on Gaylord and Pratt. These five sections were referred to as "Up the Way" or UTW, and even back then I considered them all slums.

Everybody from sections one and two went to Woodland Hills Elementary School. These two sections probably only covered a one mile radius, but it included what seemed like a billion children.

I was a very small little boy for my age, always at least a head or so shorter than everyone else. Because of my light brown skin complexion, my long eyelashes and long hair, the guys in school would tease me and call me a girl. When I say 93rd was hard and rough, I'm not exaggerating, it was hard and rough! Even at the age of five, every section was solid and had their own fighters.

In Section One we had Scoot, Bryan, Kamar, Bolo, Pig, and Ted. Those were the guys in the five through seven years age bracket. Older guys in our section included Ben, Mark, and Moe Hynsley. Marv and Joe were actually Ben's nephews, but Ben was the youngest. There was a house full of Hynsleys. They lived in a big red house next to Bizby playground, in the center of the neighborhood. Nearly every month a dead body was found at Bizby, but it was our playground and we still played there every day like it was normal.

Section Two had green-eyed Leon Ward, his little brother Onie, Ant (small, but tough), Boo, Marv and Mark Buchanon, and Boobie. Then the cousins Fingers, Lil Man, Keshante, they all could fight. I can't forget the Akbars, Brail, Sully, Wajid (the little brother) all lived on Marah. The Akbars' family were Muslim and super athletic. From Raymond, there was Allen, Tommy, and little Earl. From Heath, Tim and Marshon Davis were also part of Section Two. This section had many more streets and guys than our section, but they were our allies. We all had a silent love. We played football, basketball and boxed against each other. Maybe a fight or two. But it was love. We were boys. We were poor. It was the eighties. Everything was about sports and fun.

I went to Woodland Hills for preschool. Then, I got tested and was considered gifted so I was sent to a magnet school called Hicks Montessori. Magnet schools are public schools with specialized courses or curricula. My granny was so proud. She always wanted the best for me.

My mom left me with my grandmother when I was a year old. I'm not sure how my granny felt about that but I think she was already exhausted from raising her own children. But my granny was strong. My uncle and Aunt Gale were strong as well. I never seen any of them back down from anyone. In my opinion, they were crazy. They spoke up for themselves even if the person was bigger than they were. To me that was risky 'cause I was small. My uncle would always say, "Boy you gone be little, but size don't mean shit." He would tell me how important my respect and reputation was. I was five years old. Those things weren't important to me at the time.

Every Friday night Jimmy would visit. He was Tug and Gale's biological father. He had always been around. He would take me to McDonald's every Friday and give me 50 cents. I would buy a juice and cheeseballs or a Fudge Round and Funyuns' Chips. I looked forward to Jimmy coming. Even though I wasn't his grandson, he treated me as his own. When Jimmy came the house lit up. It was fun. He took us all to the lake every Saturday. Jimmy had money and he kept us okay. My grandmother didn't have a job or receive any assistance for me. She was prideful. Everybody in the neighborhood respected my granny. I think she cussed out every neighbor and their children at least ten times. You couldn't step foot on my granny's grass and you damn sure couldn't come in her yard. She was private and she kept to herself.

2

Then out of nowhere, seemingly my life made a drastic change overnight. I guess I was about seven years old when Jimmy didn't show up one Friday. I remember hearing him and my grandmother arguing on the phone a few days before. Then, he started coming every other weekend until he never came again.

My Aunt Gale got pregnant and moved in with her boyfriend. Her boyfriend was from Section Four. My Uncle Tug was back home from the service for good, after being back and forth for the last two years. He now had two little girls and he moved with them and his girl to be a family. The house was empty. It was just me and my grandmother. Life was boring and now I knew we were poor like my granny would always preach. But she would also say, "As long as you got hands and feet, you can hustle," and those words stuck with me for life.

My aunt and uncle still came to get me on the weekends. The street Prince is where my aunt moved with her boyfriend. That was Section Four and that street was filled with little boys my age. My favorites were Brick and Jock. Going with my aunt was still eventful. She would take me to Cedar Point, Chucky Cheese and fishing with her and her boyfriends' family, the Simmons, and I was always appreciative. My aunt and uncle would always buy me small birthday and Christmas gifts. When Jimmy stopped coming around, from the age of seven I never had another Christmas. I would go to school and lie about what I got for

Christmas. But shit, we all was lying. Wasn't no food stamps getting nobody shit!

I would walk to Mather Daycare to catch my bus to Hicks. Mather was on Union, a couple of blocks over from Gibson. That's where I met Raymone. He was a very hyper kid, a little older than I was. He was tall and slim with very curly hair. He dressed better than any kid I had ever seen. He had an older brother. They were probably three or four years apart. There I also met Larry. He was exactly my age. He was mature for a kid, quiet, very smooth and humble. He could go anywhere he wanted. He was a child/grown man. We were only seven. It was weird. Raymone was ambitious like a New York style kid. Larry was just Larry. Both Larry and Raymone were from my section. Larry lived on Union and Raymone at the top of Gibson. They were my best friends. Shit they were my first friends.

My life had a pecking order. God, Uncle Tug, then more Tug. He always took me everywhere. When he went to the service I cried for weeks. He would send me boxes of clothes and toys from Korea. Tug taught me everything. He taught me my first jab, how to shoot dice, how to shoot a gun, and how to do pushups and sit-ups. He even taught me how to wipe my butt. He was 15 years my senior. It was almost as if I was his son. I loved him. I believed everything he said. He was superman. He always came through. I had only heard stories about my uncle's physical abilities. At home he was just Tuggie, but in the streets he was "Tug". His name was strong, he always expressed the importance of family and that you have no friends.

When I was about six years old, there was a little boy on my street about a year older than I was. His name was Shon. He bullied all the kids on the street. He was loud and tough. He beat me up from the age of six until his family moved away. I would always ask, "Uncle Tug, why do I keep losing?" and he would tell me, "Always punch first." Then, I would ask him, "Well, what if he doesn't fall and still beat me up?" He'd reply, "What if the first punch is the last?" I continued to let Shon push me around until one day I did punch him first and he fell. I was so scared, I just stood there. He got up and kicked my ass as usual. But this time Tug was watching, as well as Shon's parents and my Aunt Gale.

Gale was pregnant, looking like she was about to explode. Tug and my granny began to curse and Shon's mom cursed back. It ended up with Shon's stepfather, Billy, a guy who was much bigger than my Uncle Tug, calling me a little girl. And that comment caused my uncle to lash out. They exchanged words. Billy told my uncle he would beat him up so many different ways, but Billy was with his friends and they all seemed to be a little older than my uncle. I remember thinking, "He's too big for my uncle and that my uncle was out-numbered." My uncle walked back to the house and sat on the porch. Billy stood in front of our house with his buddies.

Everybody in every household on the street came outside to watch. I was crushed. My hero didn't look scared, but he wouldn't fight. He sat on the porch and smiled while my granny made phone calls. She smiled as well. Maybe ten minutes went by with Billy calling my uncle a "pretty boy" and letting him know that he couldn't whoop him. He said my uncle was too young and too little. Then, familiar cars began to hit the corner and my uncle jumped off the porch.

Tug had on black and white Pony sneakers, green joggers and a white button down dress shirt. He wore his hair in a long Jheri Curl style. He was a very handsome guy with straight teeth. He would put you in the mind of the boxer, Sugar Ray Leonard.

Billy and my uncle squared up. They both threw good punches. He was way bigger than my uncle. After a minute of me being nervous about my uncle losing, he threw what seemed like a magic punch that knocked the bigger, ugly man to the ground. The guy was knocked out. Tug had dribbled his head like a basketball. Blood was all over my uncle's white shirt. Billy begged and pleaded with my uncle. I wasn't the toughest little boy, but I knew I would never beg and squeal the way Billy was doing. His words were, "Youngblood, please!" and my uncle's words were, "That's my nephew, my family. I will kill you!"

It took several people to get my uncle off of him. Nobody helped Billy because those familiar cars were filled with my cousins which were my uncle's age. My Uncle Ronnie was there as well. He was bigger and even tougher than Tug. He was distant, but everyone knew the "Hayward" brothers would fuck you up! That day in 1985 will always be clear in my head. The vision of Gale holding an axe while pregnant and Tug beating the odds. Family meant everything.

3

Raymone and I were both advanced and thirsty little boys. He was my type of guy. We would go to any neighborhood store and hustle. We carried bags at Pick-n-Pay, our neighborhood grocery store. We pumped gas at gas stations. Whatever hustle, he was always down, no matter the weather. We stole candy and we talked on the phone all night playing pranks on peoples' phones. We were inseparable. We both loved fashion and tennis shoes. His older brother would hip him on to the styles then he'd show me.

Raymone's mom worked for the government and I loved going to their house. They always had Kool-Aid. He was allowed to do laundry, cook, and iron. Again, he had style, his clothes were creased and he cared about his appearance at nine years old. Raymone had two little sisters. They were two and five years old and his brother was thirteen. Everybody in the house was dark skin and well-groomed with curly hair. For the next few years, Raymone and I did everything imaginable to get money. We hustled, stole bikes and anything else to make money.

Even though I hustled as much as I could, I still always wanted more at eight years old. That summer was big for me. I was leaving Hicks and going to Memphis Elementary where all the neighborhood kids who were leaving third grade at Woodland Hills were going. Larry and I walked to the Upper Cut Barbershop and I got my first haircut that year.

Everybody knew me in my section of the neighborhood. I had been going to the grocery store for my granny since age five, literally. I had a bike at that age that I rode everywhere. Not to mention that bike was the only memory I had of my mom. She showed up with that yellow Huffy. That was the first time that I ever remember meeting her and it was the last thing she ever bought me.

Besides being known as, "Them Hayward boys nephew" riding my bike, and hustling, I went to Mr. Agnes the neighborhood hardware to get help building go carts. I would use Gabe's tools. Gabe reminded me of a pimp. He stayed across the street from me, but he had a towing company as well. He was very successful. He had nice cars and even nicer women. He was tall and dark, with long, relaxed hair and gold teeth. Gabe was there my whole life. I can't remember life without him smiling and saying, "Hey Mr. Chris." Everyone loved Gabe.

Next door to me was the Top Family. Tamika and Tina Top were sisters. Their brother's name was Junior. He and I were the same age. Tamika was four years older and Tina five years older than we were. Junior was very timid. Their family were Jehovah Witnesses, but they didn't act any differently than anyone else. They were always in some mess. Both sisters were light skin and nice looking with nice shapes. I loved them both. Their father was Bart. He was a slim, tall, laid-back cat. Real respectable, but their mom was a live wire like my granny. Ms. Top and my grandmother never got along.

Across the street, two houses up is where Jack lived. He was two years younger than me but five times bigger and stronger. Jack was like my little/big brother. He was part of the Gamble family; Larry, Mac, Melba, Faith, Derrick, Red, and Jerry. There were a lot more Gambles, but Larry was the oldest. He was big, black and strong. He was a teenage superman. There was nothing he couldn't do, no sport he couldn't play and shit, he could whoop everybody's ass on Gibson, as well. He was five years older than me. He was our official artificial football quarterback as well as the instigator for all the fights.

We had a corner drugstore called Cermaks. Everybody from Section One and Two went there daily. It was in the center of everything and they sold everything. I went there five times a day to hang out with Bino. He and Rome were both from Beacon, they both worked at Cermaks and they were both about ten years older than I was, but they were the exact opposite of each other. Bino was a real handsome popular guy with a curl. Rome was short and fat, and he smelled bad. But I had known them both my whole life. Their families were close to mine. We can blame Tug for that one I guess. He wiggled his way into at least one woman's pants in every family in the neighborhood. Bino had a variety of women visitors. They all resembled black movie stars. I admired him because I thought he was smooth.

One day I came to the store to get my granny a Sunday paper. Bino was drunk, really drunk. He said, "Chris, I'll give you five dollars to put these newspapers together." It took me two days to make five dollars carrying bags at Pick-n-Pay for a dime each time. So, of course I did it. Opportunity had knocked. That day had changed my life forever. I don't think I ever touched a toy again. I began to work there Sundays through Tuesdays, and also Friday and

Saturdays. I stocked the store, put papers together and cleaned. I made $30 a week at nine years old. I was ballin'!

I was working, hustling, and waiting to start the fourth grade at Memphis. All summer long, all I heard was that Memphis was a gladiator school. I came from a major works school, all nerds, no fighting, etc. Oh, I lied. A boy name Carl McGabe punched me in the nose for breaking his He-Man toy when I was in the second grade. I didn't fight back. I sat on the school bus afraid. Going to Memphis was major. The bus stop was at the corner of my street. My grandmother walked me to the bus for the first few days and she prep talked me the whole way about not pissing on myself in school, like I had continuously did three years straight in first, second and third grade.

Memphis was different. Compared to where I was coming from, it was loud, unorganized and very dysfunctional. Raymone was already going to Memphis and we rode the same bus. I recognized a lot of faces from the neighborhood on the bus even though I didn't know all of their names. The bus was full. Everybody from Section One, ages nine through fourteen rode my bus. We got on the bus at 93rd and Benham. Even though Memphis stopped at sixth grade, we still had thirteen and fourteen year olds on the bus. They had failed a grade two or three times already.

My fourth grade teacher was Ms. Haynes. Everybody in my class was eleven or twelve and I was the smallest boy in the class by far. But I made friends with everyone. BJ, Clinton, Tony, and Roger were all from around the neighborhood. Tony was a bully from Raymond. He was much bigger than me. He wore nice clothing. I think his parents sold drugs. That was the only explanation for that back then.

Deonte was the only person in my class from my section. He was Kamar's brother. Roger was from Aetna. He was cool as well. But my best friend was BJ. He sucked his thumb, but he could draw really well. He was so tall he seemed to be six feet even in the fourth grade. Then there was Clinton he was cool, but quiet and always smiling. He could draw, actually he was the best artist in our grade.

Ms. Haynes was cool. She was short and heavy set, but a nice looking dark brown skin woman with long hair. She brought sundaes from McDonalds every Friday for the entire class. She was loud and sweet until she gave swats. I received plenty of swats in her class. But I would rather sit on a burning behind than face my granny. I never cried like some of the bigger, older guys. I just took it and sat down. I feared my granny ten times more than 100 swats.

School was fun most days. The bus ride home was even more fun. The whole bus would beat the windows and seats to make beats as the entire bus sang the raps of the Beastie Boys, Dana Dane, Slick Rick, Run DMC and LL Cool J. On the bus I always talked to Bryan. He was two years older than I was but we were in the same grade. He was loud and flashy and dressed like a drug dealer. He had two teenage brothers, Ace and Rich who were ballin' already back then. Bryan wore gold jewelry and Adidas jogging suits, etc. He was really tough, but he never tried to bully me like the other boys. Even Raymone would bully me sometimes to try to show off for the other boys.

I skated through fourth grade like a breeze. It was 1986. That summer, I chipped my two front teeth really bad. My granny beat my ass, she was pissed. She cried her favorite tune, "We're poor, your momma gone, and we ain't got no insurance." I thought it was cool because Mike Tyson's teeth was fucked up. Back then you were either Mike Tyson, Michael Jordan, Jerry Rice, or Magic Johnson. I was only good in football so I was Jerry.

I turned ten years old that summer. Then my mom popped up. But she didn't look the same as she did when she brought me the bike five years prior. She looked like she had made a turn for the worse and she had two little boys with her. They were my new little brothers, Abe Jr., and Jerry. They were three and four years old. She lived in the projects down on 30th and she seemed to drink a lot and do drugs. But I was a child happy to finally get to know my mom. However, that fantasy didn't last long. My brothers and I had a bond. It was weird because we hadn't grown up together, but we still knew we were brothers.

I was always a very hyper child. I hardly ate or slept. I lived on high octane. My granny had to make me eat and drink water. At ten, I woke up thinking of money. I pitched quarters after work at Cermaks and shot dice with the teenage boys. I was pretty independent like every other boy in the neighborhood. We played games like 33 or Down the Man every day. Sometimes we played Any Bounce. Life was good. Working at Cermaks allowed me to meet everyone. Across 93rd was a street by the name of Crane. Elmar, Lil Tony and Chunk all lived on Crane. Elmar was my age, Tony was two years younger and Chunk was about two years older. Chunk's last name was Gowens. He was very muscular and could play every sport. He was dark skin and his hair was so nappy, it looked like he had a bald head and it rained little black dots onto his head. Chunk was Crab's son. Crab was a smooth older cat, my mom's age. He had four sons and one daughter. Chunk was the oldest. The Gowens' family all lived in one house on Crane. There were probably about four generations living there, literally fifty people. Crab was cool. He walked the neighborhood with a chessboard and he always wore dress shoes. He even hooped in them. Everyone loved Crab. His smile was movie star like quality. They were so white that they looked like he had veneers, back then. My Uncle Ronnie had two children by Crab's sister, Linda Gowens. So, Chunk and I were like cousins, because Linda's children, Jamell and Tonya were our mutual first cousin. In the ghetto everybody was cousins.

4

That summer, different boys were popping up everywhere in the neighborhood. Ced moved to Cleveland from Mississippi. He was my age. A short, very athletic little boy. He was muscular built like a southerner with the accent to match. He was brown-skin with a big head, loud and walked on his tippy toes. He was very competitive. Then the Queen family; Vermaine, Vera and Vernon came from Alabama. Vermaine and Vera were twins. Vernon was a year younger than they were. They were foreign looking kids with real curly hair. Their accents were so bad that you couldn't even understand what they were saying. They were brown skin and very nice looking kids, but they were bums. They stayed next door to Larry on Union.

Then there was Dude. He was two years older than me. He came from Chicago. All the girls liked Dude. He was light skin with green eyes. He was short with curly hair. A bully. He had a much more advanced swag than us. He always seemed to be up to something. He had an older sister Kita and an older brother, Roc. I noticed back then all the boys with teenage brothers were advanced. Raymone, Dude and Bryan were all a little swifter than the rest of us.

All that summer, I would tell Larry about coming to Memphis. He was a grade behind me because his birthday was in January. My friend Kimmie. She was from Section Two. Her cousin Chrissy and I were in the same fourth grade class. I would talk to Kimmie three-way on the phone with Chrissy. They were the Markers. Boo was Kimmie's brother.

They looked like two little half Asian kids. But their nappy hair gave them away.

Chrissy was dark skin and athletic. A tomboy who could beat most boys our age fighting and run faster, as well. She even spoke up for me at times and told me to stop being a scary cat. Chrissy was my girl. She would always say, "Christian, you can probably beat these boys if you tried." Kimmie was Chrissy's opposite. She never liked conflict. She was pretty, non-athletic and a little chunky. She would come to the grocery store while I carried bags hustling, or to Cermaks to keep me company for a few minutes while I did my work. She played on people's phones with me and Larry.

I remember starting fifth grade. The kids in Memphis were robots compared to where I had left two years ago. I was never challenged mentally. It seemed like I could have been teaching the class because I had learned all this stuff in Hicks in second and third grade.

Christmas 1986 swung around and as usual I didn't get anything. I cried all day literally. My granny didn't know what to do besides say, "Shut up boy." About 11 pm, Tug pulled up. At the time he was driving a 1970 something Bonneville, the long ones. It was silver with a red top. It was super clean. He called me outside. He said, "Why you always crying?" He was drunk and In the Christmas spirit. He pulled a Huffy Sigma out from the back of the car. A Huffy Sigma was the bike of all bikes at the moment. It was a grey cheap version of the more expensive freestyle bikes. It came in grey with white disk wheels or black with black and grey disk. It was the Mongoose or Diamond Back of the ghetto. Tug had saved Christmas. And he gave me a hot wheels box. In the hot wheel box there was no cars or race tracks. The box had been resealed. It was full of brand new clothing. He said his friend worked at Higbee's and hooked him up. I didn't know or care how, I was just happy it was done. Tug always came through.

That was my second bike. My first bike was the yellow Huffy and I'll never forget that bike because it was yellow. And again, it was the only thing my mom had every brought me, as well as, my first memory of her. She pulled up in a red Cadillac with her boyfriend Abe. They looked like movie stars. My mom had a gigantic afro. She was light skin, very well groomed with a sundress on. Abe was dark skin, nicely built, with a long Jerri Curl. I was amazed my mom was beautiful like women I had only seen on TV. All of my uncles' friends always joked about how fine my mom was. Every time I heard the words, "Chris, you're so cute" from any woman, "He look just like his momma," always followed. She was legend for her walk and looks. But that was in 1982. She dropped the bike off, but didn't stick around to even see if I could ride. I had never been on a bike before. My Aunt Gale showed me one time. I jumped right on that day and rode ever since.

I can't down play Aunt Gale. She was ten years older than I was. She was more like my sister. I would cry if she didn't give me a good night kiss. She would help me sneak my toys to school. She never told on me. One time, she pulled up to my bus stop on the way to school. I was in the third grade and she took me to Cedar Point with her graduating class. Boy did we get in trouble. My granny went crazy. My aunt helped me cut school, but a trip to Cedar Point was worth hearing my grandmother's mouth.

The Demon Drop came out that year at Cedar Point. I loved Gale. All her friends would kiss me, say I was cute and call me their little boyfriend. On birthdays, Gale would buy me gifts with her summer job money. Granny, Tug, and Gale was all I had and I knew that.

My Uncle Ronnie came back from Mississippi that year right before I went to sixth grade. He had been gone about four or five years. My cousin Jamell was his son. We were the same age. Ronnie would try to keep us together as much as he could. Ronnie was tall and dark-skin with very curly hair. He was very handsome. A legend for his basketball skills. He was very competitive.

I was very skilled at playing football and for a ten year old, I was a good boxer. I couldn't win a fist fight, but I kicked ass with them gloves on. It was weird. I kept nice boxing gloves and a nice football. Uncle Ronnie would take me everywhere and put me up against older, bigger boys in every sport. I would always come out victorious. Even in basketball, which I was never good at. My will to never let him see me lose, made me win.

During that summer he came back and took me and Jamell and one other boy to Woodhill Park. We were all ten years old. He told us that whoever made it around the track one time, the fastest, he would buy them McDonalds. One time around the track was like ten miles when you're that small. I still remember him saying, "On your mark, get set, go!" We took off. Jamell and the other boy was clearly faster than I. They were taller and had better strides, but I was never a quitter. All I remember in my head was Tug saying, "Pace yourself, the horse that runs fast, don't run long." I ran at a decent pace and stayed right behind them. Half way around the track, they were both tired and had gave up and stopped running. I wasn't near tired. I ran easily to the finish line. When we all got in Ronnie's car and drove to McDonalds I ordered a fish meal. As soon as he handed me the bag his exact words were, "If you don't eat it all, I'm beating your ass." Those words ruined my victory, but that was Ronnie, well at least towards me.

5

We lived four houses up from the corner in the only pink house in the vicinity. That one big slab of concrete missing in the driveway was the most memorable image of my house growing up. Regardless of the missing slab, my granny still took pride in our lawn. She made me pick weeds, mow and cut the grass at an early age. I hated doing it, but I had no choice. We had roaches, mice, and rats, but not as bad as others. My granny was strong. She seemed like nothing bothered her. That winter our furnace broke. It was so cold, I cried for days. I could feel the cold in my bones. Granny made me put on layers of clothing and we slept under the covers together and she explained to me how cold the world was and times could be worse. Crying never fixed anything.

I don't think at that time I had ever heard my granny say she loved me or shit anybody for that matter. But she showed it. I only seen her cry when Jimmy left for good. My grandmother was stronger than any man I had ever met. My life wasn't just my neighborhood and working. I actually came from a huge family on my mom's side, Perkins/Stevens. I literally had hundreds of cousins my age. We were the Haywards. Out of my granny's eleven brothers and sisters we were probably the poorest.

My great-grandparents lived on 66th and Hough. And that's where the whole family would meet up. Not purposely, that's just where you could bump into any family member on any day visiting. My great-grandfather was from Florida. His name was Matthew. He was mean like my granny. He was short, dark skin and what he said was "law". He had that old man smell. He was a retired city worker. He was a real man. My great-granny was light skin and real pretty. She was blind. She would rub my face all the time and say, "Chris, they said you're really handsome." She baked the best rolls in the world. I forgot to mention she cooked and cut vegetables like she could see. She played the piano. Both my great-grandparents were in their eighties.

Our family had a reunion every year at what we called, "The Country". It was about forty miles east of Cleveland. A lot of acres of land with two houses that my family owned. It took all of a million years to drive there it seemed. But it was always worth the drive. I got to see all of my cousins, including Martin and Marco. They were already six feet at thirteen years old. They were brothers. My grandmother's sister Dora had fifteen grandsons my age.

Martin, Marco, Armon, Rasheed, Keith, Gerome and Chris were my favorite cousins. Keith was my age. I considered him the toughest of all my cousins. He was wild like me. You could tell he wasn't from the suburbs or his parents weren't in the military. Macy was his granny. She was the oldest of my granny's siblings. Phil and Christal were Keith's younger brother and sister. We were all close in age. I had about fifty cousins five to ten years older than me, so when I was younger they were teenagers. My favorites were Mooki, Face and Dontee. Mooki and Face were brothers. They were Bell's sons, my granny's youngest sister. And Dontee was Cathy's son. Cathy was another one of my granny's youngest sisters. NOTE: My granny had seven sisters.

When you're truly from the gutter you learn to appreciate everything. I appreciated spending time with my family at the reunions. Outside of our reunions, I spent more time with Jamell. We were the same age, only months apart. We were exact opposite. I was light, he was dark. He was tall and I was short. I had medium grade hair. He had very curly hair. He was hyper as hell. He was the splitting image of my Uncle Ronnie, his father. He was the closest thing I had to a brother and we weren't close at all. We played, but it was always competition and he could never weigh up to me but he always tried. I never believed in competing against family. Tug always preached, "Family is family." My other uncle lived by a different code that I never understood even at nine years old.

I'm ten years old, fifth grade, in Ms. Ifleen's class. She was a medium built, white woman with a short blond hair cut and glasses. She had a raspy voice and sometimes walked with a limp because her leg or foot was jacked up. She was mean and told it like it was. When she was trying to comfort a kid for crying it seemed phony. She couldn't even act nice.

Memphis Elementary was different this year. Everybody was there. Everybody came from Woodland Hills that graduated from third grade. Larry, the Queens, Kimmie, etc., and a lot of guys I expected to see that I knew were my age didn't' show up. Rasheem, Ted, Elmar and a few others. They were still at Woodland Hills. How, I don't know.

That summer, I met a lot of guys from Sections Two and Three at Cermaks. My favorite was Boo-Baby. He was from Section Three. He was very handsome. People always mistook us for brothers. But his hair was so fucking nappy it was terrible. He had a brother two years younger than him name Mista! Boo-Baby was brown and Mista was yellow but they looked exactly alike. It was weird because everybody knew Boo-Baby. It seemed like he walked the streets all day with his brother. We hit it off good. Boo-Baby was ahead of his time even back then. He was smooth. He knew how to drive, he claimed. He was only ten years old, but he acted fifteen. He was my boy. Bino liked him too. If I didn't have the job at Cermaks first, I think Boo-Baby would have had it.

When 1987 approached, my neighborhood was getting more and more loud and busy. The streets were always loaded with people. A lot of the older teens that were dirty were starting to look clean. Everyone seemed to be under Suave's command. Suave was my uncle's friend. He was a little younger than my uncle. I knew Suave my whole life. He was our neighborhood hope in every sport and he was expected to make it big. "Benny Wilson" is all you heard. He was flamboyant, tall, dark skin, and very loud. He was slim with an athlete's swag. But this summer he wasn't playing sports. He was prancing down the street dressed like Run DMC, Slick Rick, or Dana Dane. Depending on the day, Suave was fresh. He gave me $10 every time he saw me. He wore big mink coats and gold ropes. You knew when Suave was coming. He was flashy and made it known he was getting money. He would see me and say, "What's up, Lil Chris?" Everybody respected Suave, but he respected my uncles even more than people respected him.

My fifth grade year was raw. I got bullied a lot, but I met everybody that year. I got in at least twenty fights. My arch rivals that year were Teon Clear and Dennis Nowell. They were from Section Two. Dennis was a foster kid with ten brothers. Teon had a younger brother name Cam. Teon and I would always play the dozens, then he would threaten to beat me up. It seemed like him and Dennis took turns beating me up, but I never quit.

In my class from my section was Scoot, he was Bolo's twin brother. They were fraternal twins and exact opposites. They were both nicely built but Scoot was the bigger of the two. He was darker and much better looking. Bolo was short like me and ugly with a big nose. Bolo was loud and always in the mix. Scoot was laid back. Scoot was actually the toughest boy in our neighborhood. Bolo was more bark but he was far from soft.

Kamar and Bryan were tough as well. But they couldn't beat Scoot, I don't think. Scoot was a year older than I. He would always say, "Chris, you can win." He replied, "Nobody can beat me until they show me!" I liked that saying. It always stuck in my head.

6

I was the ultimate hustler. I carried bags at Pick-n-Pay, I worked at Cermaks, I pumped gas and I washed out the tub for Tug. Even though I gave every penny to my granny I felt like I was doing something. One time that year I had washed out the tub for Tug so many times he gave me $200. The first time I had ever had over $100 at one time. I pitched quarters, shot dice, etc. I began to lose respect for the guys my age who didn't at least keep fifty cents in their pocket. I always had money, and I mean always. Even if it was just a quarter for a video game.

That year, I took the test to transfer to the Cleveland School of Science. Ms. Ifleen recommended I take the test. All that time I thought she didn't like me. She cried when I passed and she told the whole class out loud that I would be leaving to go to The Cleveland School of Science. She told me she knew I was special and I was the cleverest child she had ever met. In mathematics, I was a genius. In reading, and writing, I was even better. Nothing was a challenge to me mentally. I could read like an adult and add like a calculator, just as good and fast. Even though I didn't want people to think I was less cool (a nerd), I knew I had an advantage. I knew I was swift, very swift.

Cleveland School of Science was the best of the best. It started at sixth grade and went all the way up to the twelfth. The elite children from all over Cleveland went there. We all caught the bus (RTA). I met guys from the projects, St. Clair, Superior, Westside, etc., and places I had never heard of. I saw beautiful older teenage girls. We switched classes when the bell rang. It was like I went from first grade to the twelfth grade overnight. The experience was amazing for an eleven year old. All that freedom. Catching two buses to go downtown every single day. It was sweet. The only person from my section who went there was Tina, my next door neighbor, but she was in the twelfth grade.

My first week my granny made me catch the bus with her. I was embarrassed. The next week I refused. I had caught on. I didn't need supervision. I would catch the 15X downtown, then Loop to school or I would catch the 10 across to the rapid, the 14, the 3, the 6 and the 1. You could connect to any bus from the 10. The 14 went down Kinsman. The 6 went down Euclid. The 3 went down superior and the 1 went down St. Clair. The 19 went down Miles. I liked the 10 because you would see everyone in the city it seemed. Between Cermaks and going downtown to school, at eleven years old I knew everybody.

Everything is changing. My mom came back around and she's still with Abe who is my brothers' father. Now they don't look like movie stars. They look like life had taken a turn for the worse. Every time my mom came over or I visited her, she had a black eye or a bruised arm, etc. They were always drinking (her and Abe) and whatever vehicle they had always seemed to be on its last leg. Abe religiously whooped my mom's ass. I would go down in the projects on the weekends. I had friends in the projects that I knew from school. The projects were super fun. Everything was right there, even McDonalds.

One day that summer, my granny called me from outside. My Aunt Gale was there and they were both acting frantic. We went speeding to the hospital. When we got there they took us into a room and there laid my mom. She was beaten half to death. Her whole face was rearranged. The neighbors had found her hung, but not done correctly. And she had been beaten with a shotgun. She looked like a monster. Everything on her face was three times its normal size and her teeth were missing. She had a cut across her nose from eye to eye. She was only 4'11" tall and 100 pounds. Abe had dogged her badly. That was the day I swore to never hit a woman. Because I had seen them sniff coke I thought that was the cause, so I swore to never try drugs, not even weed.

My uncles were hunting for Abe for what seemed like years. But it was actually only a week before Tug caught up with him. We were riding up Kinsman. Abe worked at the Shrimp Boat on 130th and Tug knew it. When Abe got off Tug was waiting. As soon as he hit the parking lot Tug met him with a flurry of punches. Abe was much bigger than Tug but speed was power. Abe was no match for my uncle. He began to try to wrestle but Tug seemed to meet him with a combo every time he reached to grab him.

It was a big crowd. Abe was tired and bloody. He gave up and looked like a sad pup. He knew he had done wrong. Tug got back in the car and we pulled off. The next day, my granny had received the call from the fourth district police department making her aware that 'my mom' had sided with Abe, pressing charges against my uncle. It was the saddest thing I had ever heard. Tug never went to her aid again. My mom had been released from the hospital and went back to the very person who almost had taken her life. After that I never viewed Abe the same. That's the first time I remember thinking or imagining a murder. It was weird because it wasn't because it was my biological mom, but because I knew no woman could defend herself against a man. I felt violated. She was still family, but at eleven years old I was helpless and not able or resourceful enough to act on my thoughts.

7

In 1988, Benny Wilson, DJ Ace, Mighty Stone and Pharaze (who was also my cousin Mooki) had just came down off the fame from their '86, '87 hit single, "Fresh off the Street." I was going to seventh grade. I didn't know much about the streets except for what I had heard, seen my uncle do or what I learned from Bino at Cermaks. But I did know crack was the new way to make money. I saw it on the news. It's taking over America. I'm hearing it's a form of powder cocaine turned into rock form. I also see the teenage boys in my neighborhood starting to look, act, and dress like LL Cool J, Run DMC and Slick Rick. Suave was dressing first, but now everyone was. The word on the streets was Suave had keys, whatever that was and everybody in our whole vicinity worked for him. And it showed.

At this time, I had three different crews, literally. My school crew included Bob, Ike, Marvell, John and Marcus. Bob was from Superior, Marvell from Section Two, John from Section Three, Marcus from Harvard and Ike, from Section Five. We all met on the number 10 bus every morning on our way to school.

Riding bus number 10, I met everybody from Section Three. There was one teenager who stood out. His name was Golden. Golden was tall and dark skin and he always had on the newest clothing. He was about sixteen. Everyone seemed to respect him and all the girls liked him. I would ask Golden for change if I needed it and he always gave it to me. I looked up to him. He was polished. Much different than any of the older guys from my section. I think he went to Max

Hayes Technical School. My main crew was my boys I met every day on Crane: Elmar, Larry, Chunk, Vermaine, Ced and Lil Tony. All we did was play football and basketball. Those were the good guys. Then, there was Scoot, Bolo, Raymone, Bryan, Kamar, Lonnie and Dude. Those were the bad boys, my third crew.

Lonnie was from projects, but he came to my neighborhood on the weekends. He was really tough. A pretty boy who looked soft but was the furthest thing from it. Those guys didn't play much sports. They terrorized the hood. They stole, they fought, and they were in The Folks. They were real. They even named themselves The Ruthless Squad.

I can say that all three of my crews were physically tough. I was the smallest in all three crews. Lil Tony was two years younger than me but we were still the same size. My school crew wasn't poor as my Crane crew or the bad crew. The bad crew hung on Anderson and Benham. Those were the two forbidden streets. That's where Suave hung and all the crack got sold.

It looked like a million zombies walked my neighborhood at all times. Most of these people I knew from growing up and they all looked really bad. The women looked worse than the men, probably because growing up I paid more attention to the females. Growing up, I had a crush on a lot of them. Some were my uncle's friends and some were my aunt's friends. Some I had been introduced to by Bino. But now, you couldn't tell the women from the men until you got up close to them. All of their clothes were sagging. They all had the same pale looking skin. At that age, I couldn't identify with the whole situation.

I can't lie, I hated school. But the freedom was priceless. I was 12 years old but I felt like I was doing a lot. I had a whole year of middle school completed. You couldn't tell me nothing. Seventh grade we all came back to school thinking our style has multiplied by hundreds. Ike, Marvelle, Bob and Marcus were the main crew in school. That year, Rob Dixon and Lindell came to the School of Science.

Rob was from Union. He was very tall and lanky, brown skin with full lips. He was really silly. Lindell was a short, but wide and although he was about two years older than I was we were in the seventh grade. He was real dark and to me he was not handsome. But all the girls loved him. They loved him to death. He was from St. Clair. He was hustling back then. It was 1988.

Even though our school went up to twelfth grade, I honestly felt like we were the most popular guys in school. It seemed almost as if the board of education purposely put together a crew of the smartest, but wildest young men from all the worst neighborhoods.

Back home in the neighborhood we had a new addition to both crews. Ron Heart moved from 79th to Union, on 93rd in the Cermak Building. Ron had a sister, Dominique and two little brothers Lil Berry and Jim. They were all Chinese looking like their dad Berry. Berry was cool. And Mrs. Heart was the sweetest woman ever. She was the cool mom whose house you could go over at any time and eat or sleep. She didn't care. Ron was two years older than me, but he was a perfect addition to the crew. He was a little taller than I, about a shade darker, and a few pounds heavier. But Ron was down. He could play every sport to the highest degree of the word. But he was really quiet. He rarely ever said a word. I hadn't seen much of the bad boys since I had left regular school. They hung out on Anderson and Benham. Sometimes, we would play football and basketball with them and from time to time everyone came through Cermaks. I was almost always there.

During that year everyone started learning to box. A guy in our neighborhood name Tank taught us. Tank was in his late thirties. He cut a lot of the guys' hair in the neighborhood, while talking the whole time about whooping ass and killing people. He was loud but for some reason I believed his stories and that he would whoop ass. Tank had two sons. One my age and one a little younger. Tank was poor. He was getting by the best he could. He was short and athletic built. I would consider him a decent looking guy with salt and pepper hair. For the most part he was cool. He would let you pay him later for a haircut or slide if you were short. He stayed in the littlest house on 103rd between Benham and Anderson. It seemed like the house only consisted of one room and the front porch where he cut hair. Tank was one of the first men I considered worthy of respect, outside of my Uncle Tug and Bino.

It seemed like the crack was taking over. That's all they talked about on the news. My neighborhood was infested. Every time I went outside my grandmother would holler, "Chris, you bet not go on Anderson!" I would laugh and walk to Crane where we played sports all day. I could usually always be found either on Crane or at Cermaks after school.

My Uncle Tug had moved back home, he and Tiny had broken up. I couldn't understand why. They seemed like the perfect couple. Plus, Tiny was the finest chick to ever come from my neighborhood and that was weird because she was known for whooping ass. Tiny had three sisters, Pam, Trina, and Rose. They were Bino's first cousins. Bino had two brothers, Glendell and Linnie. I can't forget Lai-Lai. She was bow legged. A black African queen with a gap in her mouth. Pound for pound they had a family of stacked up brick houses and they were all loud and tough. Tug and Tiny would kick ass together and sometimes he would kick her ass. Tiny was like family. In my mind she was my auntie and I had a crush on her. She had green eyes and the biggest, juiciest lips ever. She was one shade from light skin. Her and Tug laughed and played. I thought they were what couples were supposed to be.

This year was a great year I thought. Crane went undefeated that year in football. We beat everybody from Kinsman to Rawlings to the Ruthless Squad to Section Two. Some teams we beat twice. Everybody was playing for Pal 6 football. I tried out and made the team but the day I got my equipment Pig from my section beat me up in front of everybody so bad after practice that I never went back because I was embarrassed. I slowed down visiting my mom and brothers because of what Abe did to her the year before. My mom was fully recovered. Besides losing a few teeth she was back with Abe doing the worst.

My Aunt Gale worked for the city and so did Tug and Tiny. That's why I was puzzled about why he moved back. They both even had matching new cars. A Pontiac Grand AM and Pontiac 6000. They lived on Ansel with my two cousins Janice and Sasha. They seemed to have it all. But Tiny would complain to my grandmother that Tug had begun to use too much of that new drug and began to act weird and crazy.

As 1989 approached, I was still doing the same stuff but I had begun to migrate more. I would hang with the guys who hung out on Anderson more. Raymone and I still hung tight although he was a little more advanced. He was stealing his mom's car picking me up and we would joy ride. We would go on Kinsman to visit guys that he knew.

On Kinsman was Black Dre. He was really dark-skin with very white teeth. He was slim, about my height and he had a big block head. Then there was Boots, Roy Koole and Sammy. All three of them were very tall to me. Boots was dark skin and silly. Roy was my complexion and had NBA skills as a teen. And Sammy was a tall, well groomed, baby faced kid. All three of them were two or three years older than me. Raymone introduced me to them.

If you had any kind of basketball skills you knew Raymone and he knew you. He could dribble and shoot. Whatever he saw Michael Jordan do he caught on and copied. He could hang with the grown men at 14 on the court. He played from sun up 'til sundown. I would just watch him and gamble on him. Raymone knew what was going on everywhere, rather it was who had the best gear, who was boosting, where the parties were, or what shoes were coming out. The only video games we played were Tecmo Bowl, Double Dribble, and Contra. Even though I hustled with Raymone and we had a lot of fun. He looked down on my Crane crew, but I was closer to them. Larry was my best friend in the world. He had a mind of his own, while Raymone did what the crowd did.

That year my grandmother started working at the Justice Center, so we had money coming in. I could tell Tug was hustling because I was stealing at least $40 to $100 a day and he never mentioned it. I'm not exaggerating, I stole money from him daily.

One night I was half asleep. I heard the door slam and it sounded like Tug and my grandmother talking, so I creeped down the stairs to listen and I saw Tug drop into my granny's arms and cry uncontrollably. I heard him tell her how he couldn't stop getting high on crack. I was crushed. My hero, my superman, my everything had been defeated by something the size of pebble so small that if it was a rock on the ground I would refuse to pick it up to even throw at a car.

Tug was the glue to our immediate family. He was a real man. I watched his appearance go down. He got smaller and smaller. He would wear three outfits at once to disguise his weight loss and he would smell the entire upstairs up. He always seemed mean and his skin looked a mess. I vowed to never drink or touch a drug to sell or get high on. I didn't think money was that important after watching my uncle go down. He went to jail that year for a short while and things got back to normal again. At least he wasn't getting high.

That summer while my uncle was gone even Suave began to look different. As well as all the guys he had under his wing. My neighborhood was full of what looked like zombies. I mean it was rough. Crack was King. There were rows of bushes that you couldn't see through, but if you walked inside there were couches and crates set up and tables and beds like real houses. Inside there might be thirty crackheads smoking. You had the Animal House on 98th and Benham. There were drugs being sold out of it daily, all night and day.

Before Tug went to jail my granny would walk up there to find him every night. It was sad because she wanted her son to just come home. Nobody could understand why my uncle couldn't put the drug down. I watched her cry and stress over Jimmy for years. Now the same process had begun all over again. But this time it was for the love of her son. On most occasions, I would walk with her on her journey to find my uncle. Sometimes it would be 2 or 3 am. Granny didn't care. It was so many people out that it seemed like daytime, so we felt safe. Everyone respected my uncles and my granny as well. We could do as we pleased, unharmed. We were never successful getting Tug home. He would run when he saw us. I actually didn't think crack would stick around, so it wasn't too serious to me at the time.

I'm working at the drug store with Bino. He started to have way more clothing and jewelry. He was fly anyway. Now he was wearing the expensive Lotto, Troop, MCM, & Fila jogging suits. I think he was selling crack as well. Shit! I know he was but he still had a level of respect for me and wouldn't expose me to it. But he was my boy. He taught me about condoms, getting Crabs and getting burnt and what to look for in a chick. He taught me what to say. He would always tell me I was handsome and I would get all the girls. I loved Bino almost as much as Tug. Bino was family. Rome was family as well but only because his family was close to my family.

That year I began to steal from the cash registers at Cermaks and I always managed to make it look like it was Rome. Cermaks was owned by whites and employed all white workers, except us three. I learned early how sneaky some white people were and that no matter how close you were to one or how much they benefited from you. They always thought that they were above us and we were less clever. But I didn't mind because right under their noses, I just played the kid role and I kept what I needed (for free).

I supplied my whole crew with candy, chips and whatever else from the age of nine until. They never seemed to miss a dollar or an item. They were rich white business men making money off of pharmaceutical drugs in a ghetto full of poor blacks. Bino would always say, "Take that shit, they can afford it." And that's what I did. It was smooth. I got big holiday bonuses and whatever my granny needed.

That year Tug was released. I'll never forget. He came home from Mansfield. He wore a bright ass yellow Adidas jogging suit. It looked silly but it was Tug. I didn't care what he wore I loved him. He was big and looked real healthy, but believe it or not he was getting high the same day. He looked smaller in what seemed like three days later. He called me to his room and said, "Chris, I raised you. Don't do as you see me do." In his firmest voice he said, "You're better than me. Drugs are for suckas. I'm being a sucka right now." He went on to say, "Weed is the gateway drug" and I believed him. I always listened to him because he always had a true story to back up his theory, and it usually was somebody I knew or their family that suffered the lesson so I could see with my own eyes.

Tug never sugar coated anything. He always tried to build my confidence as well. That year he told me, "You're handsome with charm and charisma." He always stressed that he didn't want me indulging in all the activities that all the other guys my age were starting to indulge in. At the end of 1989, my Uncle Tug got shot in the head trying to rob somebody. I was playing football and I saw the ambulance passing Crane speeding to Benham. Then the word made it to us (my boys) and we began to run to Benham. By the time we got there the entire neighborhood was there and Tug was laying there just about lifeless. I knew I would remember everything he taught me.

8

My life was never the same. I vowed to never hustle. All the boys my age would come to Cermaks and say, "Chris come to the block," and I would say, "Naw, I'm cool."

In school Lindell and Marvelle were selling rocks and they kept them in Chap Stick containers. Raymone, Bolo, Duke and Bryan were all selling crack, but I refused. That winter, R. Kelly and the Public Announcement came out. I was walking down the street in my brand new red, Triple Fat Goose that my granny bought me with a fur hood and Bino pulled up in a brand new Mazda. It was gold with tan leather interior. It was a stick shift with a sunroof. Bino was always fly. He had leather racing gloves on that matched the interior. The gloves with holes everywhere with the straps on the wrist, unbuttoned. He said, "Lil nigga, get in." I jumped in and smiled. He said, "you don't know shit bout this". Then he blast the radio and all you heard was, "dedicating this one to my favorite girl she's the only woman in the whole wide world." It was a smooth tune, but I thought it was the same guys who made "Let's chill" but Bino said, "That's R. Kelly. That nigga nice". To me all slow music was the same. He was an Aaron Hall sound alike to me. We rode up Union and we kicked it all that day. All I remember thinking is, "Bino ain't making all this money at no damn drug store (smh)." Everybody was selling crack.

When I became a teenager everything became a question mark. "Should I do it or shouldn't I?" That's the stage when I wanted so bad to be doing what the big boys were doing but I was still in a small boys frame. I still loved sports and just being a kid. Peer pressure never affected me. All the guys I had grown up with were starting to drink 40's and smoke weed.

That year everyone joined the Folks (GDs). My Crane crew was honestly stronger than most boys physically but they were looked at like jocks. That year, Cordell moved over there from Hough. He was real big, husky, dark skin dude. He lived on Union in Fat Breon's old house. It was on 90th and Union across from Gaines funeral home, a red brick house that stood out. One day while walking past the house we saw a kid that seemed to be about our age playing basketball in Breon's old driveway. He didn't look familiar and he had a hoop on the garage. We all got excited, but didn't approach. I walked in his yard and said, "I'll play you for a dollar" with all the confidence in the world and he accepted my challenge. That was the entire crews' invitation inside. I ask him his name and he replied, "Cordell." I looked at him and knew I would beat him due to him almost being fat. Cordell beat me every single game. He beat me so many times by the time it was over it was dark outside. In fact, we all loved him and his whole family which had come out to watch us play.

Cordell had an older brother Michael. We didn't see him much because he was ten years older. His sister Leacia was two years older than him with hips and a butt like a grown woman and his little brother Danny was about seven. Nita was the mom. She was short, really fat, and loud with a squeaky voice. I quickly became her favorite of the bunch. We all loved Nita. She played spades against us for money. Until this day I think she cheated because we never, ever won. And I mean, never! Cordell's dad was Big Mike. He was tall and slim. Cordell looked exactly like him. The whole family was extra dark skin. Big Mike was an alcoholic but he worked every day. He was a real man. He gambled with us while drunk in a game of dice and talked shit until we all left upset and broke. But he was cool.

Cordell had a well-rounded family like Elmar and Ron. In the hood, well-rounded just meant the father was in the home. All the rest of us were ass out in the daddy department. Larry's dad was there but Larry lived with his grandparents. We had fun that year. Our team was strong. Cordell was the Bull Dog's star linebacker when he lived on Hough. He had trophies everywhere. Everyone knew to stay away from Cordell with the football. We would all go to VEL's Nightclub on Sundays from 7 pm until 11 pm. That was the teenagers' night to shine. Everybody from twelve to eighteen years old was there. Jerseys were hot that year and all the different color Filas and Cortez Nikes (dope mans). Everything was colorful.

That year Dale moved to our neighborhood from Garden Valley projects. He was my age, a little shorter than I was and very wide with big feet and hands. He had a big nose and he was ugly. He was tough as nails. He was a Bensol. His whole family were bums and I mean bums. He had two sisters and a lot of cousins. Von and Cori and their sister Angela. Dale's sisters were Nina and Shontel. They both had hazel eyes like the mom. They were all step-ladder in age. The girls were actually pretty but they all looked like slaves and never wore shoes. Dale was dark skin. Everybody else was brown but they all favored. Dale would meet us all in the playground and he would be barefoot playing football and basketball in rocks and glass. He was so good in basketball I named him Muggsy Bogues, after the real short NBA player and everybody followed and shortened the name to Muggsy or Muggs, and we never heard the name Dale again.

Everything was poppin' in my hood. Tug was out of the hospital back on the block. Suave and Rob Long were robbing everybody on the block while getting high. Now I'm rotating crews. Sometimes I hung on Anderson and sometimes I hung on Crane. I had begun to steal mountain bikes and sell them. I was still pitching quarters in school and working at the drug store. Everybody my age or a little older had adapted to the crack thing and had begun to make money. Kamar, Bryan, Bolo, Scoot and Dude were all hustling. They all looked like guys from the movies. They were clean. Bryan even had a car. They would always ask me, "Chris, you scared to get down?" and I would always answer, "Naw, I'm cool." Raymone was hanging with them. I think he was making a little change as well.

That year Dude got caught and sent away for a year and a half. It was unbelievable. I would always think, gosh he's actually locked up…wow! I couldn't imagine being away for one day. I would always ask Kita about him. Even though he bullied me, I considered him my friend because we grew up together. I was still very small in size. All the other guys were growing taller and wider. It seemed I never grew. I was actually discouraged. Everybody was even having sex and I still didn't have hair on my dick yet.

In the very beginning of 1991, I was fourteen and I got expelled halfway thru the ninth grade. I wouldn't be attending the School of Science anymore. I would be continuing high school at John Adams. My grandmother worked from 5 am until 4 pm, so everybody who cut school came to my house. We would have a ball. I didn't have to be at Cermaks until 4:00, so I had a lot of free time. The boys start arriving at my house at 7:30 sharp. Both crews. The Crane boys and the Anderson boys. We would gamble on Tecmo or Super Tecmo. We also shot dice. My house was safe. All the girls came over. It was fun. On warmer days we would throw rocks at police cars and make them chase us because we were truant from school. It was a rush. We would go up to other schools and throw eggs in the schools and run. Nobody ever got caught. The police patrolled my neighborhood hourly. There were so many drugs being sold, it was like a Harlem movie scene all day. I stayed on Gibson, the safe street. The street you ran to when u got chased by the law. Once you got off Benham and Anderson you were safe. Orleans wasn't hot as Anderson and Benham either. Those streets were on the news daily. But I always thought, "What's so bad about it? I know everybody walking my neighborhood. They're just doing the drug now." I still spoke to what seemed like 1,000s of my moms and uncles' old friends every day. I had known them all my whole life. I was very popular due to being around the corner at Cermaks, I knew 90% of the people that came in the store or got off the number 15 and the number 10 buses. I was, "Little Chris".

One day Raymone and I were just sitting around. It was early in the morning. I'll never forget the day. It was April of 1991. I had just seen New Jack City. He approached me like Gee Money approached Niño in the movie. He said, "You got any money?" and I told him "Yeah, $20." He told me that I could turn that into $40 or even $50 in two minutes.

I asked him, "How?" even though I already knew what he was going to say, but scared because I knew, I would say yes. It was Raymone. Every move I made I did with him from the age of seven. He said, "Let's go up on Anderson." I was scared but I knew everybody, so we left and walked up Gibson to the 96 street cut across from the Hynsley house and thru the alley by the side of Anderson store. We were on Anderson. It was exactly like the movie I had just watched. Anderson was divided into two sections. You either hung on the bottom or the top half of Anderson. Both halves were controlled by different sets guys ranging from ages of older teens thru early twenties. The guys on the bottom had more money. The guys up top had money, but they were grimy. They robbed and killed and sold crack. They were more vicious. I was cool with everybody on both halves. Strangely, Bryan managed to fit right in with the older boys. He, Scoot and Kamar all had a spot among the teens and older boys. It was crazy because these guys were in my grade in school. The guys my age hung out by the store. It seems they were catching the left over money. But even the left overs seemed to be a hell of a lot. The store was owned by Cross, the Arab. He would let his favorites come in the store when the police came. It was weird because nobody ran when police came. They only ran from vice. They disrespected regular police. I had never seen anything like it. They cursed, stuck up their middle finger at the regular police. The guys up top would even shoot at the helicopters in attempts to knock them out the sky. These guys were wild. This was nothing like Crane.

Raymone and I walked to the top half. It was like I had been recruited from high school to college basketball. I got a bunch of warm greetings, "What's up, Lil Chris," was all I heard from both sides of the street like I'd been late to a party that had been going on for days, and I was the last one to arrive. The older guys at the top were Tez, Frank, Phil, Fray and Bay-Bay. There were more players, but those were the majors and they were all balling with fresh cars. Frank and Phil were brothers. They were short and looked exactly alike. They were brown skin with large gaps in their front teeth. They were cocky from down south. They both talked really fast. Tez was from Houston. He was dark skin, tall and slim, loud with a Houston mentality. You knew not to fuck with Tez or he would kill you right there. Fray, tall and dark skin, had a rep like Tez but wasn't as hard. He was more bark to me. The rumor was that they both had multiple bodies, but Bay-Bay was the hardest of them all, in my opinion. Or maybe he was just the ugliest. He was short, dark skin with big lips and he was really cut up. All of them wore big chains and saggy jeans. They all wore, Used and Girbaud jeans. They all had Cutlasses and Monte Carlos with 10" Seven Stars. Phil was the flyest. He had leopard interior in a gold cutlass. Tez had a drop top Monte Carlo and Fray and Bay-Bay each had a '79 Cutlass. All of them had Seven Star rims. But Frank, the oldest of them, rode Astro Vans and newer cars than them. I think Frank had the most money.

That particular day, I walked up and they were all outside. I didn't even know what to say or what to do. Raymone told me to ask for a dub. That was short for a double up. So I did. Everybody liked Lil Chris. I was the size of a ten year old. But I was sharp. I had worked at Cermaks for years and I wasn't the average 14 year old mentally. Tez called me to the side and said, "Give me that $20." I'm thinking, "Hell naw!" Then he pulled out a gigantic pill bottle. It was full of white pebbles. He poured some in his hand. They all seemed to be systematically cut exactly the same. He explained, "These are $20 chops," and Phil chimed in, "They either get a 20, a 10, or 3 for 50." Then Tez gave me four of the pebbles that he described as 20 chops, and a smaller one which looked half the size of the 20 chop, a 10 chop. He said, "Come to me when you need a dub." Phil said, "Stand right here." The cars were pulling up like a McDonald's drive-thru. I could look down to the bottom half of Anderson and see that the traffic was just as heavy down there. Phil would yell, "Lil Chris, this you!" I ran up to my first car and it was a $20 sale. I made the fastest $90 I had ever made in my life. And I was with the big boys. I was nervous but I felt safe. Safe and making money. The next day I went and cleared my bank account of my last $70. This was way better than anything I had ever seen. I swore I would never hustle, but the money came so fast it didn't seem like what the news made it out to be. Everybody was either using it or selling it. I quickly started to want what the older boys had. And I wasn't stopping until I had it.

9

All my life in school, at home, on the news etc., all I ever heard was how bad it was to be a street guy. I never viewed myself as that. My first few weeks selling crack was amazing. I would hustle from 6 am, as soon as my granny left for work, until 4 pm when it was time to go to Cermaks. I left the store around 7 pm and I either went to Crane or Anderson. But I was slowly beginning to leave Crane all together. I would beg my Crane boys to come sell drugs on Anderson. But they weren't interested in the money that bad. And actually, they weren't allowed. Anybody couldn't just make a friendly stop on Anderson and make money. You had to be an original or from the five streets in our section.

My first few weeks I made money. I begged all the junkies not to tell my Uncle Tug. He mostly came out at dark. We still met in the house. I thought he had no clue that I was selling crack, until one day I was coming out the bushes and he was on the corner and he seen me. I was caught, I couldn't run. He said, "Chris, get yo ass over here. What you doin' up here?" I retorted, "Nothin." His answer to my short response was, "Don't nobody come up here for nothin." He then proceeded to enlighten me on how he'd been watching me slingin' crack for days and just didn't want to believe it was me. I begged him not to tell my granny. He swore he wouldn't, but he let me know that we were in no way, whatsoever, finish with the conversation.

After my encounter with my uncle, whenever a junky wanted a free jolt they would threaten to tell my grandmother I was hustling, and I always paid up. I wasn't as scared of getting' in trouble as I was of crushing my granny's soul. I just didn't want to add more hurt to what she had already been going thru with Tug concerning this very issue.

I quickly abandoned sports. If I wasn't at Cermaks, I was hustling full-time. I was buying quarter ounces for $200 soft or $225 ready. Ready meant seven grams, already cooked. One weekend after a football game for some reason Muggsy wanted to fight me and everybody knew it but me. After the football game the crowd was following me home. It was a mixture of the Bad Boys and Crane. When we got to my house my granny was outside. Boo-Baby and Muggsy had begun to hang out together. When my grandmother came out Boo-Baby and Muggsy told her I had been selling crack. I couldn't believe it. Even though we were children I always knew to never tell. Tug taught me that at three years old. My grandmother asked me if what they were saying about me was true and I told her that it wasn't. She said, "If it ain't true you'd better whoop somebody ass for lying." Muggsy and I squared off. We fought long and hard. His main objective was the slam. I always used my hands. He talked and slapped his chest most of the fight. I stood text book and nervous but we fought. He slammed me finally and my granny broke it up. That day Mugs became my arch nemesis.

I continued hustling. Tug would school me daily. He told me, "Once you pick this side of the law, ain't no turning back." He told me that if selling crack was what I truly planned on doing, then I should aim to be the best crack dealer in the world." Even though I felt that my uncle was talking stupid to me for some reason, when certain situations approached, his voice constantly played in my head. For instance, I clearly remember when he told me that I didn't have any friends and that this was a dirty game. I remember when he told me some of the guys I knew would go to jail, some would get killed, some would go crazy, and some would be gay. He also told me, "One will be you," and that was the scary part. But the scariest thing he told me was, "The only thing the streets respect is violence and murder." I was only fourteen when he told me this. I didn't even own a gun. At that time I was 5' 3', 105 pounds, not hurting nobody. I just wanted to make money.

Anderson was ruthless, and that's an understatement. It was the slums for real. But it was normal to me. On Anderson the junkies could beat the dope boys. We had Big Les who would squint his eyes a million times and you knew you were about to get your drugs took. Big Les was one of Tug's best friends, so I never worried about him. Most of the junkies were still cool with my granny from child hood. She moved on Gibson in 1966. We were one of the first black families in the vicinity. So history was sort of respect as well. My granny asked me daily, "Chris are you selling drugs?" and I would say, "no granny, them guys are lying." But they had already planted the seed in her thoughts.

Hard cut Levi's Girbruad, Tommy Hilfiger, Used and Damaged were the hot clothing. Real dope boys wore Air Raids, Mowabs, Hurachis and Jordan's only. That was the summer of 1991. The movie, "Boys in the hood" came out year and Jodeci was the hottest new tune. You copped your dope from Gina or Ray C, if you needed weight or other heavy weights from other sections. Getting crack was never a problem, but I wasn't buying more than a quarter ounce regardless. My program was buy quarters and save the profit.

I quickly built my clientele. I didn't look at this as a career. I just wanted school clothing and a fresh car with some deep dish (10" wheels) like the big boys then I planned to stop. Tug would always say, "Selling dope is just like using it." Y'all wear y'all clothing for days without eating and sleeping, just like us." He would tell me, "Chris, I can't stop you 'cause you're addicted, but I can teach you what you need to know." He would sarcastically end every sentence with, "What do I know? I'm just a fiend."

Anderson was like a true organized crime field. Every dope house had a razor and a plate on the back porch. The last nigga to cut his dope, put a fresh three pack of razors back there. The dope men with weight rode thru every hour and dropped off weight. The dope was so potent you knew it was A1 as soon as you opened the bag, the smell was so powerful. Some junkies like yellow some liked white. Sometimes you would get a grey or brown batch. But it was all cream. Gina sold chops for $20 that you could cut three rocks off of. It always made me curious how she made any money. The first time I met Gina she refused to sell me dope. She said I was too young. I was with Bryan. She thought I was ten years old. I proudly told her with my chest out, "I'm fourteen." She asked me if I could count, and then sold me my first quarter ounce. She charged me $190. I thought I had made a major move, thinking, "I get to cut my own fuckin' rocks. Wow!"

One day that summer right before school I went back on Crane and played football in my $100 Mowabs and messed 'em up real bad. But it was cool to escape the madness of the block. I was comfortable back with the good ole boys. Nobody was in competition about clothing or cars, etc. No police, no guns. It was all love.

10

When school started that year the whole School of Science crew transferred to the public school in their section. Bob was from Superior, so he went to East High School. Ike went to South High, Lindell went to Glenville, Marcus went to Kennedy and Marvelle and I went to John Adams. Believe it or not, Rob Dixon killed somebody and went to jail. We were all fifteen or sixteen. We all split up but never lost contact. I would go on Superior to my aunt's house and kick it with Bob. One weekend while Bob and I were walking down 84th and Superior, I pulled out a pill bottle and explained to Bob what crack was and how to sell it. We walked around all day saying, "You straight? You straight?" I even bought a dub from Dude, his next door neighbor. I introduced Bob to crack. I knew he would excel. He was savvy and sharp as myself. Bob was a pretty boy with real curly hair. He had a younger brother named Eon and the finest momma in America. Bob & I would call each other every day to report our progress. We were both moving rapidly, but I must admit that he caught on faster than I expected. We were both getting a lot of money.

John Adams wasn't anything like The School of Science. It was like the movie, "Lean On Me". One big ghetto fashion show. My hood was one of the top hoods. Everybody from Section One thru Section Four went to John Adams. Everybody knew Anderson niggas was getting money. If you got money you were considered, "Rollin'." We were all rollin' ass young niggas and most of us could fight. I wasn't known for fighting. I was a small pretty boy. But if you messed with me you would surely get your issue. I lost every fight in the hood, but my crew wouldn't allow me to lose anywhere else.

I was a new face at Adams. All the girls talked about me and Boo-Baby. Even the twelfth grade girls would flirt with us. I had study hall with Golden. I hadn't seen him since my early School of Science bus days. He was about eighteen now. In Adams, he was King. He hung with Bumpkin and Lil Tee. These guys were teens getting money but not our kind of money. They were selling and fronting out weight. You could get ounces and even eighths from these guys. Tee had a Sterling. He drove me home every day. He would front me two ounces for $2200. He would complain that I took too long moving the dope.

Golden was the leader and commander of where they were from, which was East 102nd. He was the face. All the girls liked him and every nigga knew and respected him. Even the jack boys and murderers. That was the first guy I ever looked at and thought, "That's how I wanna be."

I didn't have a car at the time like some teenage players. Like my dude Brick from over on Prince. He had a Box Chevy with 'Ride the Rhythm' written on the trunk. Him and Jock had come a long way. They both came from large families on Prince. I'd known them since my aunt had moved to their section when I was six years old. They seemed to have caught on to the crack wave very well. They were both short, athletic built. Jock was brown skin and had a baby face. Brick was dark skin and looked more rugged. They were a great duo.

My guy Rick from 131st was a few years older than me. He stayed next to the Boys & Girls Club and always managed to have a car even if it was a junkie's car, he always had a car to drive. He would take me to Durkee to hustle. Durkee was a lot like Anderson but it was on the Main Street. A constant flow of traffic. Traffic in any hood meant big money. Even though that wasn't my section the guys welcomed me because of Rick. Rick was a tall slim guy that thought every chick in America wanted him. He wasn't a bad looking guy and he did have a lot of chicks. But that's all Rick talked about Girls, girls, girls. Rick was about 18. He was Sammy and boots age. Rick had hustle. But he didn't act his age.

One day walking down the hall I saw what I thought was the finest crew of chicks and they were fly. One of the girls shouted out, "Hey boy, ain't you from Anderson? Don't you hang with Bolo?" I shyly responded, "Yes." I wasn't supposed to be shy. I was a fly dope boy. But I was on a new playing field. She introduced me to her crew. It was Jin, Ranita, and another girl whose name I've forgotten. The girl introduced herself as Sheena. She was brown skin and looked Indian or Rican. Her hair was down her back. She was slim and real pretty. We exchanged numbers and began to talk on the phone daily. A few weeks after we met, she called me at 7 am while I was getting ready for school and asked if she could come over. I told her that she could and she arrived about 8. We both were cutting school. We talked and laughed.

Sheena was cool. We popped in the bootleg VHS tape, Boys in the Hood in the VCR. Halfway thru the movie she cut it off and put in a Levert cassette tape. All I remember hearing is, "Baby I'm ready to give you all of my love girl. I'm tired of playing games/so many girls I can't even name." Rope a Dope Style was the name of that tape. If you were playing Levert or Jodeci, you were a winner with the girls. Everything was moving fast. I looked up and Sheena was taking off her clothing. I was more nervous than when I was about to fight somebody. I'm sure she could tell. Once she got completely naked I explained to her that I was a virgin. I was embarrassed. She told me to take my clothes off. I refused. She told me to get under the covers and get naked so I did. Then she directed me on top of her. I had only heard stories about sex and seen it on movies. Let all my friends tell it, they were all getting pussy.

I had heard stories about girls drowning guys, meaning they had small dicks. I had never even put too much thought into sex, but before I knew it she had put me inside her and she moaned out real loud. She grabbed my ass and I instantly felt violated. But that was her way of guiding me. I quickly caught on. Off course we stayed in one position, which was missionary. I was nervous, embarrassed, excited. At that moment I think everything you can possibly feel except hatred went thru my body. Then I felt like somebody was tickling my whole entire body and I got a crazy sensation and it felt like I pissed. Then I felt a relief I had never experienced. I held her tight and she looked over at me like I was a little boy and said, "Don't worry, you just nutted." We had sex nearly every day after that and I told everybody. When I say everybody, I do mean everybody.

For the most part Adams was live. Raymone & I were two of the best dressed teens in the school. We were fresh every day. We probably didn't wear the same clothing for thirty days. One day Raymone said, "Chris we gotta get them new boots all the older niggas wearing." I asked, "The boots with the wheel or the tree on the side?" He said, "Yeah, those Timberland boots." Back then, Timberland had about six different styles. The black or butter constructions or the two-toned cloth, light or dark brown. The orange and green ones with the big tongue or the Super Tims, which were $350. Only the big timers wore them. Raymone wanted them. And he had a plan to get them.

I had just learned how to drive. We had a red Pontiac 6000, a junkies' car. Raymone wore his Boston Celtics starter coat and I wore my Alabama Crimson Tide. He explained that there was a shoe store on Chagrin called Ed Nova's, and we were going to rob the place. I was scared. It was Shaker. We had stolen bikes and sold crack, etc., but a robbery in Shaker??!!! I couldn't imagine. We planned it all day. We mapped it out ten different ways until finally the time came. We rode up Kinsman without license. He drove 'cause I wasn't a great driver. We parked behind the plaza and went into Ed Nova's. We were clean so they didn't expect what was about to happen. Raymone asked to try on the Super Tim's and I asked to try on the pair I wanted. We both walked around like we were excited and were very interested. Then Raymone pulled out the gun and ordered the lady to empty the cash register. I had already made my way to door just in case they could lock it from behind the counter. I held the door open an inch. Once Raymone got the cash he began to run towards the door. Once he was out we took off. We ran fast as we could until we heard sirens everywhere. We laid down next to a car and said, "Ain't no use of giving up now." I told him to give me his coat. We crawled to the car. He laid in the back seat and I drove slowly from behind the plaza. I was petrified. It seemed as if everyone in every car that passed us were looking inside our car. I drove the speed limit as the police came from every direction. I didn't make a mistake with any turn signals. When I passed over the 140th Union Kinsman split I knew we were safe. My first robbery successful. Raymone was pumped. We split $800 dollars and we both had new Timberland boots. In our minds, we had won.

11

For better or worse, I didn't know. But I was changing.
I would stand on the corner of 93rd at Cermaks and claim
every car I would have one day, when I grew up. I liked the
5.0 and the SS Monte Carlo. But to me the car of all cars
was the big body Benz Coupe. I didn't know what they were
called, I just knew it meant status. That and the two door
BMW. Didn't know the name of that car either. I only saw
those type of cars in videos and movies. I quickly erased
getting those cars out my head. Even though I thought
positive I thought that was thinking ridiculous.

  Gina had the new Acura Legend and Ray C had a Blazer
and a convertible Trans Am. Gina even had a Convertible
Iroc. They were stars. D-Bone and Cheese were from
Section Two. D-Bone had a Benz 190 and Cheese had a
mouth full of gold. They supplied Section Two. 1992 rolled
around. The group, Das EFX came out. A Tribe Called
Quest and all the weird rappers like Leaders of the New
School, Pete Rock & CL Smooth, etc. KRS One was fading
out. 2PAC – Violent, was the anthem now. DJ Quick and
D.O.C were all the shit. Every car you passed seemed to be
playing one or the other.

  One day we were all on the block and the vice hit.
Muggsy and I just happened to run in the same direction. We
ran long and hard. We both ditched our pill bottles. We were
captured and unfortunately the officer seen where the drugs
were thrown. They brought the drugs to us while we were
laying on the ground cuffed and asked whose drugs they
were. Muggsy yelled out, "It's all mine." I was shocked as
hell. But the police didn't buy his story, they took us both

down to fourth district. I was later released, but Muggsy was on Juvi papers. So they kept him.

I sat in the fourth district for what seemed like a million years, waiting until my grandmother came. When the officer said, "Christian Hayward you can go" and started to open the door, I wanted to say, "Please, just let me stay" in fear of my grandmother. Now the speculation had been proved. When they walked me out, there stood Tug and my grandmother. My grandmother slapped me really hard and we got into the car and rode down 93rd to Gibson from the fourth district. I knew I was in trouble. But mostly I felt like I had disappointed my granny, but more than anything I was pissed. I had just bought a half ounce from Porky one hour before, and that was close to all I had. But it was 1992, a time when you could bring out $20 and grind up to $1000 every day if you had the hustle. Money was falling out of the sky.

Spring was approaching. Over the winter Mac and Bryan had been locked up and they both were released. Back then you could kill a nigga and get six months. Even though I had my run in with the law, jail was the furthest thing from my mind. All I thought about was hard cut Levi's and Girbruad jeans, Jordan's and trying to get a car and a Herringbone chain.

By now all the junkies were on my side. 'Lil Chris' meant something on the block. I kept good dope. I accepted $3 and $4 dollars when others wouldn't. Ben and Suave would always tell me, "You're going to be the greatest hustler ever." I didn't understand why they always said that, but it sounded great. They had both fell from the top. They were junkies. They were ruthless. They took dope and raided stashes, but not mine, I was Little Chris. Plus, Tug had always taught me during my little short career to treat junkies like people, not junkies and they will love you. "If they need it, just give it to 'em." So, I did and they never forgot. When the $100 and $200 dollar sales came they brought them to me. Junkies listened to other junkies. There could be 100 niggas outside hustling, but junkies trying to cop took the word of the junkie that was outside with the hustlers. We called them runners.

I was so cool even when I had little rocks or the worst product (quality wise) than other dealers, the junkies would still vouch for me as having the biggest and best. Crack dealing was easy for me. A lot of my dudes took a lot of losses, but not me. Tug taught me to never put my hand inside of cars, to never give up the dope before checking the money, to absolutely never get in the back seat of a junkies car, and to always carry a gun. I followed those rules, 75% of the time.

Raymone and I met on the block with baseball bats every morning at 6 am and I was always there on schedule. We never carried guns 'cause we were already cutting school and the vice cops always came unexpectedly. We hid our rocks in potato chip bags. You couldn't leave any dope at home. The morning rush was from 7 to 10 am. Then again from 1 until 6 pm. Then came the all-nighters. But I couldn't dare pull one of those.

That year every single individual was buying at least two ounces. All the dirty boys were clean. Muggsy was even clean with a big Herringbone hanging around his neck. We

were on top as a whole, the "ANDERSON HUSTLERS".
Scoot had a LeSabre. Bolo had a Grand Prix. Muggsy had a
Grand Prix. Bryan had a newer Blazer with a remote control
sound system that we had never seen. When he hit the
corner in that truck I thought, "How the fuck did he get that
off?" Bob had just got a Blazer as well, but not one as new
as Bryan's. Bryan was the Baby King Pen and we all knew it.
The entire 93rd knew it. He wasn't even eighteen years old,
playing with $50k from robberies and crack. One time I went
broke and he gave me an Oreo box full of rocks. It was
$5,000 worth of chops and I owed him $2500. He was like a
Mentor in a strange way. He was the richest one of us all.

One morning I was on the block when I saw a curly
haired, Mexican looking dude. I knew he was black but he
had a long ponytail and he was super clean. I recognized
him as the teen legend. His name was Nando. Rumor had it
that in 1989 or 1990 he had mistakenly received a package
that was meant for his Jamaican next door neighbors, which
contained two kilos. They killed the guys they thought
robbed the package and Nando had it all. I was only twelve
years old at the time, but I remembered his cars. He had a
pink Iroc, a truck with Lambo doors, and Dayton rims and
that was 1989 or '90.

One particular day in 1992, Nando made me aware
that he had just been released from prison after serving
eighteen months. He would be out there every morning with
me from that day on. We talked and walked around together.
He schooled me. He was wise for nineteen and he was
always positive. He seemed to always speak everything into
existence.

That year a drought came. Quarters were $300. Ounces were $1200. I didn't care. My attitude was as long as I make $75 dollars profit off of a quarter. Tug had always told me, "The game was the quick flip and drugs weren't legal." I had met so many people I never had problems getting dope. I knew all the older guys with weight from other hoods. I knew Fade, Golden and Lil Tee. I was allies with Boots, Sammy and Black Dre, and I could also cop from my boy Bob. It was weird that I introduced Bob to crack and I was buying dope from him. We would meet down town and he would sell me an ounce or two. I was in the game. I hated not having dope. I stayed determined.

I still stole and worked at Cermaks. I even sold dope on that corner. The Arabs had bought out Pick-n- Pay and named it Bi-Rite. And that's where I met Rick. Arab Rick owned Bi-Rite. He would give me dollar for dollar for my food stamps that I received from junkies. Rick knew me from making the money drops for Cermaks. I would take the money to the money exchange, the bank, etc. I learned early that relationships and networking were more important than the actual money itself.

I don't know how it happened but one day I only had a little over $100 dollars to my name. But I had my name, and that was a lot. I was the young hustler who stayed out all day and never left. I woke up one morning and took a gamble. It had to be around 8 am. It was March or April and it was chilly outside. It wasn't a winter day, but a rainy day that let you know spring was coming. Not too cold but not warm. I figured I would ride my bike to Ray C's house. He lived on 104th and Benham. He was the man. He sold everything from kilos on down. He was ruthless. He would repossess guys' cars who owed him money. He would front guys dope and come right back and rob them. He was the worst, of the worst. He lived right in the hood. He didn't give a fuck and everybody knew not to fuck with him. He was about 5' 8" and 190 pounds of all muscle. He looked exactly like a monkey. He was dark brown with the funniest southern voice. He was always loud and flashy. He was ignorant. He smacked guys and spit on people. He had a militant, workout constantly mentality. His house was a hang out. He wore rings on every finger and big gold chains. He wore boots every day even if he had on shorts. He was a hell of a dresser. He was very unapproachable. But I gambled.

I rode to Ray C's house and knocked on the door. His girl opened the window over the back door. She was topless. I ask her for Ray C. She shut the window and about 30 seconds later he popped up. He said, "Lil Nigga what the fuck you doing in my yard this early, in the rain?" I replied, "I need action." He asked me if I was the Lil nigga from Anderson who be outside all day and I responded, "Yes". Then he told me to wait right there. So, I stood in the rain for what seemed like an hour. I was drenched when he finally arrived and dropped two bags out of the window. They were large bags of coke. More coke than I had ever seen or held. I quickly put both bags in my red Gap hoody pockets. I didn't know if he was high because everybody knew Ray C smoked water (PCP). But he didn't seem high. He said, "there's two-eighths of keys in those bags." He explained that I owed him $8,000 because it was a front. I knew nine ounces would get me $18,000 rock for rock. So, I agreed to take the work. I rode off nervous. I couldn't believe what just happened. I had nine ounces of cocaine.

I rode my bike to Raymone's and we sat and figured out a game plan. Then, I took the whole nine ounces to Crippled Bo's house on Anderson and asked Suave to cook it for me and he did. Everybody stood around me like I was Tony Montana. It was a house full of people. Nobody tried anything funny because I made sure I told everyone who I got the dope from, plus I was Little Chris. I hustled my ass off daily and Raymone helped me. I paid Ray C off in a few days. We developed a bond, which was weird 'cause he never raised his voice at me or threatened me like he did others.

Ray C would give me eighths for $4000 and I would take them, even though I knew I was getting overcharged. I was making a lot more money without spending. He even started to front Raymone as well, because of me. But their relationship was short. He would page me every day about Raymone's whereabouts and complain that Raymone owed him. Raymone had a clothing addiction, but one day Ray C's patience had worn thin and he beat Raymone up really bad, in my house. I felt bad but there was nothing I could do 'cause Ray C was my connect and I'm sure he would have destroyed us both. He left my house and called later and asked me did I need any money to replace any items that may have been damaged in my granny's home.

I continued to hustle. Nando had resurfaced the way he said he would. He had a peel back top on a yellow newer style Bonneville with Dayton's. The car was yellow with a burgundy top. It was fly as fly could get. Nando wore wife beaters, a Herringbone and a pony tail. He was smooth and he carried a TEC-9 in plain sight. He smoked water as well but he was more mild-tempered than Ray C. Nando had eighths for $2800 to $3200. I wasn't stupid. Ray C had helped me but I wasn't about to keep cheating myself when I didn't have to. I gradually started copping from Nando. Things were smooth. He never ran out. He fronted me as well, and if I was short he didn't care.

Verts Nightclub opened that summer. Vels was still poppin' but Verts was on 131st and Miles and was geared more toward the street teens. All the gang members and hood rats hung there. All the boys underage with nice cars were there. It was live as hell. So we would go to Verts on Sundays, instead of going to Vels. Somebody always got shot at Verts or fights broke out, but it was better than anyplace else that the teens had in Cleveland.

12

My hard work finally paid off and I finally got the Monte Carlo that I wanted on Five Star KMCs. It was brown with a tan top and it was very clean. I had to keep my car on the next street so my grandmother wouldn't find out. One morning when I went thru Gabe's yard and jumped the fence to get my car, it had been badly vandalized. All of the lights and windows were busted out and every panel looked like they had been beaten with a bat. I was crushed. I had worked so hard for this car. I started crying. I felt defeated. I had no clue who would do this to me 'cause I didn't believe I had any enemies. I went to the block and me and my boys all rode back around there in disbelief. The whole block swore we would kill whoever did it.

A few days went by and I heard that Fat Rome that I worked with at Cermaks, had teamed up with the Peace brothers' to vandalize my car. I had parked my car in front of the Peace' house. I couldn't believe it. Rome and the Peace brothers were all a lot older than me. I couldn't understand their motive. They had all watched me grow up. Back then, I never understood the power of jealousy.

Suddenly, Tug's voice played in my mind, "Jealousy is worse than hate." He would always say that. When we heard the news about who had destroyed my car, the whole block piled into three cars and we went around to the Peace' home. I knocked and Ms. Peace answered the door. She was a sweet older lady who had always treated me as a nephew. I asked for her sons and she said, "Tommy is here." I said okay and I waited for her to get him. He came out and greeted me like we were closer than ever. "What's up Lil Chris?" I pulled out the 9mm that Tez had just handed me and I asked him, "why?" He was speechless. Looked like he was about to cry. He had nowhere to run. I raised the gun to his head. I did more talking than anything. He said, "I'm a ho, to any man with a gun." I was scared to shoot him. Tez asked me if I wanted him to shoot him. I said, "no" and we left. I still felt defeated.

The next day I was on the block. It was early. I was on my regular morning shift and Vice swarmed the block. I ran in junkie Russell's backyard and stashed my rocks. It was about a half ounce. I ran back to the front and tried to walk like I hadn't done anything wrong. I wasn't truant because it was summer time. When they checked my pockets I had $1,000 cash and about $500 food stamps. They knew I was up to no good. They kept searching until one of the officers came out of Russell back yard with the half ounce I had just threw back there. They took me down and charged me. I waited all day to see if the DH would accept me. I thought they would let me go like last time but this time I wasn't so lucky. They kept me. When I heard I was getting transferred I remembered all the stories I had heard about how rough DH was. I was instantly petrified. I'll never forget that day, putting on that blue suit, being sprayed after my shower for lice, putting on that spray deodorant and being walked to my pod, 2B.

Every little boy looked tough and ugly. It was so noisy. The boys who were being disciplined were in the box. That was a small cell right before you went into the pod on each floor on the right hand side. So this is 22nd, is all I kept thinking. That was the year they had begun to bond everyone over to the adult system for all serious crimes, mainly the sixteen year olds. I was still fifteen and my crime wasn't serious, so I had nothing to worry about. The only familiar face I knew was Clark Davis. He was a seventeen year old dude from Section Two. He was small but he was a dog. He was a little taller than I was at the time, my complexion and athletic built. I knew him from school and 'cause he hung with my dudes Bolo and Bryan from my section. We hung out every day in DH, always doing push-ups.

While in the DH, I met Tyson from Cedar, aka Peanut. He was the hardest little boy ever. He was super black and really cocky and he could box. He was Jamaican. We quickly hit it off. We were the same age. I also met Jerrod McCray aka Jay Rock/Super Jay. He was tall and dark skin, a real handsome guy with perfect white teeth. He was from Quincy and rumored to hit like a train.

Another guy I met, Djuan Bollard, was from St. Clair. He was only sixteen and he had killed somebody. He was the first kid I ever seen get bonded over to the adult system. Last but not least, there was Bernard, a short fat dude from Cliffview. He had a big nose and did not look like he could fight one bit, but Bernard was the dog of all dogs. These were my dudes. I was the smallest, but I didn't have any problems. Everybody else had already been down the road. They would all say, "Don't let nobody play you crazy. Punch the first nigga and everybody will be scared of you." I was thinking more like, "I'll just keep my mouth shut and mind my fucking business." But shit, in my mind I wasn't going down the road so all that junk didn't matter. I was being released at court.

About a month went by and I finally went to court. I was prepared to go home with my granny. I couldn't wait. It was August of 1992. The judge spoke her peace and asked me did I have anything to say. My granny spoke her peace, then I said I didn't have anything to say and the judge said the most harsh sentence I had ever heard. It seemed like she said it in slow motion, "One year Ohio Department of Youth Services." I waited to hear suspended sentence but after she said, "Your personal belongings will be turned over to your grandmother." I looked over and my grandmother hollered at the top of her lungs, "Nooooooooooooooo, not my baby!" That hurt me worse than the sentence. I said, "Granny, I'll be okay." She said, "Boy, I love you." That was the first time my grandmother had ever told me that she loved me. I felt I had disappointed her badly. I felt like I failed her. I went to the pod in shock. I knew I would be transferred in forty-eight hours. "Was this the life I really wanted?" I had begun questioning myself.

They woke me up at 6 am. It was crazy 'cause Clark had been ordered to wake up as well. We were about to ride out. This particular group was going to Mohican and Maumee. I heard those were some of the easier camps. They weren't like Tico, Indian River, or Cuyahoga Hills. When these three camps were mentioned for ride outs, juveniles would literally breakdown crying, out of fear. Those were the rough places.

I got on the bus and we were there an hour later. The driver was cool and even stopped at Taco Bell and gave us our last free meal. When we arrived at Mohican it didn't look like jail at all. The boys were free. There weren't any fences and the boys had on real jeans and polo type shirts. When we got off the bus we were approached by Mr. Bowen, (I think) or Bogar, a staff member. He was an Ex-Navy Seal he bragged and he told us the rules of the place. He showed us that we were deep in the woods and we could try to escape but we wouldn't make it.

Mohican was four big dorms with double beds. There were about 200 boys on each unit maybe less. The walk to the dining hall was a small stretch maybe 100 yards.

Mohican looked like cabins. It was more like a youth camp. There were boys there from Toledo, Dayton, Cincinnati, Columbus and other smaller cities in Ohio. Cleveland and Cincinnati were always the strongest and then came Columbus. One of the dorms was full of boys who were on their way home who had already done a long time in the rougher jails. Those guys were older, eighteen-twenty years old. They all seemed to be cocky and the guys in Mohican feared them because they bragged about being in places like Tico and Indian River. Clark and I kept to ourselves for the most part. After orientation I was transferred to C Dorm in the back. It was for the bad, younger boys. I had just turned sixteen.

In only thirty days, I'd accumulated so many tickets in Mohican for stupid stuff, but my stay there was a blur. One day I was awaken to find out my status had been upgraded from minimum security to medium and I was being transferred. I wasn't scared this time because we were treated really well in Mohican and I thought wherever I was going would be the same. We had everything. I didn't get into any fights. I thought, "Wherever I go the boys will be my age. How much worse can it get." I thought that all the bullshit I'd heard was exaggeration. I would be fine, I thought. The transporter told me that the bus was going to

Cuyahoga Hills, school for boys. It was actually in one of Cleveland's suburbs. I envisioned a smooth ride, a lot of visits and cheaper phone calls. For my last ten months I would skate through easily.

I arrived at Cuyahoga Hills. When I went in I noticed that all the jobs were being done by the youth. Cuyahoga Hills was the exact opposite of Mohican. This looked like what I had seen on television. It was all bad, and I mean all bad. It was noisy as hell. Every boy in the place seemed to be on steroids. I didn't care if they were tall or short they all looked like athletes. Half of them had Afros and braids and they all had a mean mug as a face. It was a mixture of shirts of different colors. The boys either had on red, blue, yellow, burgundy, green, or sky blue. Every dorm had their own color. On intake you wore grey, if I'm remembering correctly. The staff here were Mr. Allen and Mr. Jafee. The Hills was rough. I mean real rough and I was scared. There were no guns here. I quickly observed that every juvenile here strictly lived off of respect. The Hills was split up into two sides, four dorms per side. The south side and the north side. A-D was on one side, E-H on the other side. F Dorm was intake. A Dorm wore blue. The worse dorms were A, C, and H. I prayed not to go to either.

C Dorm was for the younger, wilder guys and it was actually the roughest dorm. They wore red. The day they called my name to go there I could have shitted on myself. There was a brawl on C Dorm every day. All I could think about was seeing the C Dorm guys in the hallways and hearing about somebody up there getting their head bust daily. I thought, "God why me?" I kept remembering boys saying, "They let you fight on C." I had never won one fight in my life and these boys looked way harder than the boys I grew up with. I was doomed. I walked down that hall with my laundry bag with my belongings in it, as slow as I could hoping they would tell me it was a mistake, but it wasn't and they never did.

I arrived on C Dorm. Ms. Roster was on staff. Other staff members in C Dorm were Smit and Bigs (I think). An older nice-looking black lady worked on third shift with Ms. D. I didn't know one person on the dorm and that was weird. I thought I was famous. These boys were from DTW, which meant any project from Garden Valley down to 22nd. Some guys were from Cross Town, that meant Hough all the way to St. Clair and some were from the west side. Back then, being from the Westside meant you automatically had to prove yourself. I was from UTW, any street from 93rd to Lee Road from Buckeye to Miles.

In jail, your hood meant something but your city meant everything. I was 216 area code so I was quickly accepted. On my block was Bat Mic, Haywire, and Marsheen. But my main running buddy was Andrew Pen, from Akron. He had been to jail several times and most people knew him. He was 5'7", real cocky with huge big arms. He was dark skin looked like Johnny Gill. He was quiet, but he would talk to me all day about previous bids. We did push-ups and swore we would hang out once we were released. My time began to fly. He told me to never gamble. But one day I did. A guy from Cincinnati named Roger Robins. He gambled me for choice trays. I didn't even know what choice trays were. He beat me gambling, but he never mentioned that I owed him. I was totally naive to the ways of jail. I had been called bitches and hoes and pushed on a few occasions, but I never retaliated. I just let it ride out of fear. In jail everything was about respect. But I just wanted to go home and hustle. Reputation meant nothing to me.

One morning, I was in the breakfast line and we were having my favorite which was sausage gravy over toast. I couldn't wait to eat it. I grabbed my tray and sat down. As soon as I sat down Roger Robins grabbed my plate and put it on his tray and walked off. The whole dorm was looking and I just sat there. Forgetting that we even had gambled, I don't think I would have fought even if he wasn't getting the tray for the debt I owed. He had disrespected me in front of the whole unit. I just sat there hungry. I weighed 110 pounds. I was 5' 4". Roger was one of Cincinnati's top dogs.

I was cool with Raymond Tall and Griff from Cincinnati. Everyone from Cincinnati all sounded country, most of them had gold teeth and they all claimed to know how to box. I could box a little so I knew a boxer's poise and movements, but it wasn't helping because I didn't have the heart to match. Every day Andrew would tell me that the guys looked at me as soft and I had to change that. One of the older guys, Josh Mann from Cleveland, pulled me to the side and said, "How long you got?" I told him that I had one year. Then he said, "Nigga u from the land. You better stop letting these niggas disrespect you. You making us look bad!" I just listened as he explained how I would continue to be bullied my whole time in jail. He explained the importance of not letting a Nati, Dayton, or a Columbus nigga dog me. I felt him but I was scared to even try.

A guy named Twin from Dayton would call me a bitch or a hoe every day. He was light skin with hazel eyes much heavier than I, and a little taller with large lips. I had never did anything to him. Amongst his crew, he wasn't a major figure so he used me to boost his confidence. One day on the way to breakfast it was quiet. All eighty youth were in line and for no reason, Twin put his finger in my face. I moved my head but he kept going. So I removed his hand and said, "Man, I don't bother you. What is the problem?" At that moment it seemed as everything started to move in slow motion. He called me a bitch and from the angle I was standing, I could see Mann and he looked at me and winked. All I could remember next was hearing his Tone Loc voice saying, "You never know what you can do until you try and niggas respect a nigga who will fight before a nigga who can but won't." I swung my right hand across and hit Twin directly on his chin like textbook perfect and he fell to the ground. He was dazed trying to get up. I had only seen my older guys in my hood do that. It was a clean knock down. He wasn't able to fight.

The staff broke it up and it was over. I had a small bit more confidence but not much. But things did get a little easier for me. I kept working out and chillin' with Andrew it was going fast. I had about eight more months. The holidays were approaching. It was the first time I was away from my family.

Cuyahoga Hills was gladiator school. On C Dorm it was two fights a day. I had a few friends from Columbus. Timberland was a smooth cat. He was my age and they said he was a good hustler on the streets and his photos looked like he was. He looked exactly like Dennis Rodman. Also, from Columbus, was a real short dude name D-Brown. He was much shorter than I was, but he was tough as nails.

Looking at him sometimes made me want to be hard. He had all the respect in the world. He was real silly but everybody knew he meant business if the war jumped off. He always hollered "Short North!" I guess that was his hood.

During that time Cincinnati had a kid name Carlo Strong. He was a tall, dark skin, ugly, weird looking, and lanky kid. He resembled an alien is the only way to describe him. He always talked about boxing like he had won the golden gloves. He didn't look impressive but his crew respected him. Watching all the fights and growing up in my hood I learned that looks meant nothing and to never underestimate anyone. One day he cut the radio off while everyone was listening to it. Nobody spoke up. I was standing with Andrew Pin. For some reason, Carlo and I caught eyes. He hollered out, "What the fuck you looking at?" I'm sure he thought he was choosing an easy target. But if an off brand (out of Cleveland) nigga beat a Cleveland nigga he got big props and it was rare. I didn't respond, but he started to approach me like I had disrespected him. I was nervous. He grabbed me around my neck and began to choke me. Several youth as well as Andrew broke it up. The staff ask me did I want to let it go or fight. The whole dorm was watching. I couldn't back down. I had already beat up Twin, what did I have to lose was my thought. The staff made everybody move out the way and we squared up. He threw all types of weird punches and did a lot of talking to intimidate me but I stayed in my stance and moved slowly in a circle. I always fought textbook and at my own pace. I watched him as he jumped around like Parnell Whittaker. He swung constantly missing every punch then finally I threw a perfect one-two, twice and all four punches hit him directly in the face. From that point on he transformed from a boxer to a swimmer. He put his head down and went wild. I stayed in one spot and threw a million punches until he grabbed me and I put him in a choke hold as he went wild like a bull. But he couldn't get up. They broke the fight up and it was blood everywhere. His face was covered in blood. It was amazing. I couldn't believe it. But the crazy thing was that I felt bad for him. They rushed him to the hospital. The staff made the dorm aware that I had broken his nose. He came back that same night and his eyes were closed shut and he looked like a raccoon. I can honestly say I didn't think anything of it. It was only two fights. That didn't match the 40 fights I had lost in my hood growing up. That's when I figured out that East 93rd was the jungle and these boys couldn't survive where I came from. Everybody that was in Cuyahoga Hills from 93rd that were in other dorms, were having the same victorious outcomes, when they fought.

The whole institution had heard about what I did to Carlo. The older boys on A Dorm would salute me. I had total respect. It was clear. The twins, Brad and Bill were there as well. They were two notorious brothers from Benham. We had met in the hood, when we were about ten years old. They were both light skin with curly hair, a little taller than I and about two years older. But they were down. They weren't the best fighters but they would fight and fight hard. They always made it known they had my back.

I started to notice that I had a lot more fighting skills than most boys at Cuyahoga Hills. I was a thinker. I fought my own fight and to be small, I packed a very unusually hard punch. I was also starting to grow. I was now about 5' 6", weighing 125 pounds and I was cut up pretty good. I was like a small boxer. In my book, I thought that only real ugly boys could be really feared and known for fighting. I just wanted to get by. At the very end of 1992 a guy came from Dayton named Ron Burrough. He was loud and really big, like a grown man. He hollered all day, "I'm R Bo." The youth from Dayton and Cincinnati all feared him.

I had developed a habit of wanting to see the boys with all the mouth, get into just ONE FIGHT, not five or even two. Just one. Usually the guys who talked and talked and talked lost eighty percent of the time. R Bo was my complexion and looked like a big duck with a George Foreman build and Afro to match. He had an unusual hairline. He was stocky, not muscular, but with a shirt on he looked good. But without it, he needed work. In Cuyahoga Hills, if one youth did anything the whole dorm was punished. We would sometimes have to walk the halls for hours. Sometimes we had to stand by our beds all night and sometimes we had to box and drop for hours.

Box and drop meant stand in a military style stiff stance, with your arms in front of you. When the staff said, "box" we got in our stance. When they yelled drop we stomped and dropped our hands to our thighs all in one motion. When eighty guys did it at once, it was loud like thunder and even though it was punishment it was actually live. It was organized like a band.

This particular night we were being punished, standing by our beds all night. It was noticeable that Ron had been dying to prove himself. The dorm was silent. He yelled across the dorm, "Lil nigga you think you hard because you beat up some of my homies?" I didn't respond.

I was silent. Everybody listened as he preached directly to me like Martin Luther king about how he would leave me bleeding in my draws. We all had on our draws, might I add. He swore he would kill me. All this was for him to prove to the dorm that he was hard, I thought to myself the whole time he was talking to "little ole me". He was at least 5' 10" and weighed 190. I was scared. Andrew swore if he hit me we would jump him and every other Cleveland guy said the same, but I had more confidence in Andrew. He was actually tougher than my Cleveland homies. Not all of them, but most.

We finally went to sleep and woke up like nothing had happened. We went to breakfast and as normal we had pancakes. Andrew and I sat and laughed as usual and what happened next happened so fast I could believe it. Ron walked past my tray and put his finger in my food while walking past and said, "ho ass Cleveland nigga." I don't know if it was God or if my legs had wheels but before he could take one step further I was up and I swung the hardest right hand that I ever had swung in my life and knocked R Bo silly. He dropped his tray and fell. I didn't rush him because he fell to one knee and had already began to get up. I was so mad I went at him fast but still very text book, "hands up elbows tucked" and I slid in right up under him. Like most boys without skill he began to swim. I remember feeling a real hard punch hit me at the very top of my head but I threw an upper cut and a hook and R Bo had hit the ground flat on his back really hard. He jumped right up but it was too late. The whole dining hall had begun to chant "216 216 216". He was bleeding badly over his eye and Ms. Roster broke it up along with another staff member. The dining hall was packed. Lil Chris had represented for the land once again.

That was the first time I sat and thought to myself, "I am a dog. I vowed to never tolerate any disrespect from any human being and nobody would ever beat me again. Size don't mean shit and big talk means even less." One conversation with Josh Mann made me aware of my abilities and for that I knew I would never forget him and I would always be grateful.

I was sixteen, but I wasn't all mouth. I was a natural fighter and that I would really have to prove because that weekend I called home and my grandmother was crying. I said, "Granny what's wrong". She said, "They called me a few days ago and said you're being transferred to maximum security." I said, "Uh uh, they would have told me." She explained, "They didn't want u to beat anybody else up." She said that they told her that I was a violent youth and I was too much for Cuyahoga Hills.

I had whooped ass but I was a little nervous. I knew I was going to Tico or Indian River. Indian River was supposed to be the worst. I was moved to A Dorm until my transfer. William Spence and Dewey ran the dorm. They were about eighteen years old and they were both dogs. They respected me because I had put in work. They told me to stay hard no matter where I went and I knew in my heart that I would. I liked the new me.

A few days after Christmas in 1992, I was transferred to Indian River. The boys on intake were much bigger than me. But that fear was long gone. I knew that I had a punch that wouldn't fail me. I knew I would swing first without words. Tug always told me, "The first punch could be the last, so always swing first." I was actually humble about my skills because I hated bullies and I hated guys who always talked, lost and got embarrassed.

13

When I arrived in Massillon where Indian River was located, I had all types of feelings going through my body. I was kinda anxious to see if all the things I heard were true. The first person I met there was Ms. Tab and Mr. P.

Mr. P was the exact replica of the cop Martin played on the Martin Lawrence show, but he wore fatigues. Ms. Tab was a short lady with dark brown skin. She was plain. Nothing special about her. She dressed like an old lady but she was probably only twenty nine or thirty years old and she had short hair. She wasn't mean or cool, she just went by the book.

The first guy I met was B-Oats, from East Cleveland. He reminded me of Superman. He was tall as hell and could play basketball like Michael Jordan, literally. He was dark skin and athletic built. I say he reminded me of Superman because he had perfect teeth and he wore glasses. He was handsome, but looked like a real nerd. But If he put his Index finger to the center of his glasses to place them on his face correctly you knew you were about to get dunked on or get your ass whooped like when Clark Kent changed into Superman. Otherwise, he was mild mannered.

I met the Hamland family from Youngstown. The first one I got cool with was Velt. Their whole family was in there. They were all high yellow with curly hair and resembled the Debarge brothers. My favorite youth was from Warren, OH. He's name was Alondo Kerbie. We were the only two sixteen year olds in Indian River. We were the same size and same complexion. All Alondo did was smile. He threw temper tantrums like a kid, but they knew not to fuck with him, so I guess he was as hard as he said he was. Actually, I had never heard of Warren or Youngstown, but those boys were really hard, in my opinion, due to the fact that they all had murder or serious shooting cases, and they talked about it like it was nothing. Indian River was where all the juvenile lifers were.

Every dorm was named after an Indian tribe; Shawnee, Apache, Chippewa, Iroquois, Erie, Navajo and Sioux. Erie and Sioux were upstairs. They were the absolute worst of the worse. Cherokee was the military pod where you went to complete the program to be placed back into normal population after behavior issues. Navajo and Shawnee were for the older laid back youth who were going home soon. Iroquois was just orientation. Indian River was like the penitentiary for children. Steel weights, real tackle football and guys had two for one stores. It was the real deal.

I broke a white boy's nose on intake for saying, "yo momma." I wasn't there thirty days before I was transferred straight to Cherokee. Indian River was different than Cuyahoga Hills. These boys in Indian River were much cleverer than the juvenile criminals I had encountered at other places. Most of these youth had both money and cars when they were free. They were more laid back (the majority of them) and they mostly had very violent crimes. What teenage boy thinks to kidnap someone, is all I use to think because several of them had that type of charge.

At night the staff would play music to calm us. That year, Toni Braxton came out along with H-town (Knockin the Boots) and R. Kelly came out with 12 play. SWV and Escape had dropped as well. It was a great year for music but not to be locked up listening to it.

It was 1993, I met a lot of guys from all over town. I was reunited with D-Bay. He was a stick-up kid/murderer from Hough. I had met him when I was about thirteen while visiting my aunt on Superior. D-Bay was short, dark skin and slim. He never worked out and he moved very slowly, never saying much. D-Bay's name was "Gold" in the streets. Then, there was Butch from 79th. He was shorter than me but really, really cocky and he wore thick bi-focal glasses. He was my complexion with large features, but he was nice looking with curly hair. Everyone respected D-Bay and Butch. They were both about two years older than me.

Big Rayvonne Callohan from Cedar, was a big gigantic teddy bear. Tall and fat, Rayvonne was always joking and laughing. My boy Tito, was from Union, a couple of blocks up from my section. Tito was a weirdo to me. He was tall, cocky, and light skin. He could be vicious, but he was usually quiet and humble. He was always right NO MATTER what. Then there was Spikey from 131st. He was high yellow with funny teeth and he was real loud with a Mike Tyson squeaky voice. Spikey was wild, country and ugly, known for robbing cells and always in trouble. He was just a menace.

Freak Z, was probably the hardest of all the guys that I've named. He was taller than me, slim and dark skin. He looked like Martin Lawrence but with bigger lips. Freak Z was from the lower end of Superior. Everyone knew he had go. Lastly, there was Mann Buttons from Parkwood. He was a tall, broad shouldered kid with light brown Chinese shaped eyes and a big nose. One time Buttons and Freak Z got into it and they knocked each other out about two times each. They were at it for about a month straight.

Indian River dorms were made up of two man cells. There were twenty four cells on each dorm, twelve on each side of the hall. I was close to leaving Indian River and going home. I wrote girls. I did push-ups and back arms off the bed. I had transformed totally. I was about 5' 7", 140 lbs with a huge Michael Jackson type afro.

I didn't have many problems in Indian River. Cleveland fought Columbus and a big white boy name Drew Hunter, busted my nose. B-Oats had named me Mighty Mouse after I broke the other white guys' nose and that name stuck with me until I went home. Freak Z and I fought right before I went home in front of everybody. I was out matched but we fought long and hard. Honestly, he wasn't all that I thought he was. I had underestimated myself. My punches were sending him back as well. He was older and a significant amount bigger. We didn't stay mad at each other long. We actually found out we were cousins.

It was August 1993. I'm scheduled to go. It was a journey. I was seventeen. It was a badge of honor to successfully make it home from jail in the ghetto. It was sad because a guy getting out of jail received more props for being released, then he got for graduating high school or coming home from the service. It was weird but true. I talked about kickin' it with some of the guys when I got released, but I knew that I would probably only kick it with Tito. He was on what I was on, and that was hustling. I could tell by his demeanor that he was all about the money and he was used to having things. Tito was only one year older than me but he seemed much older. All the other guys were from across town or had a very long time left, so the day I left is where I left them.

14

A Timberland boot full of rocks untouched just like I left it. When Aunt Gale and I pulled up in the driveway from the long ride home from Massillon, I jumped out the car while it was still rolling. My granny was on the porch smiling. I ran up the steps and hugged her. We were both equally happy to see each other. My next step I ran up to my room to see if everything was still in place. Tug went to jail right before I did so I knew everything was where I left it. I thought about hustling my whole time in jail. I wrote down my plans every day while preparing. I wrote down the cars I would have as well as the type of rims. I had things all figured out. I was seventeen now. In jail, I promised myself I would do a lot of things different and kickin' it with more girls in my spare time was on the list.

I was still mingling with the same females that I did when I was twelve and thirteen years old. Kimmie and I remained very close. I took her virginity and told everybody and she never gave it up again. Then there was Cee-Cee, light skin, slim and looked like a baby doll. She was almost perfect. She had short hair. Her and her mom were identical in every way, except their complexion. Her mom was brown skin with light brown eyes and just as fine as Cee-Cee. Her mom's name was Selina and she stayed in Cee-Cee's business like she was one of the girls. She always reminisced about her high school days. She could talk all day. Cee-Cee lived on 138th and Union, so it was always easy to get to her. Rob Dixon had introduced us when we were about twelve years old and they lived right down the street from each other.

Then there was Neeka. She was dark skin and slim, with a cold shape. She was Lonnie's little sister, a Stigans. The Stigan's family lived right on Anderson. But Neeka, Lonnie and Laneer lived in the Garden Valley Projects with their mom. They all came UTW on the weekends. Neeka and I were the same age. Sometimes, I would walk all the way to the projects just to see her. She was not the best dresser, but she was the epitome of fine. She didn't need clothing. She had natural beauty. Neeka looked a lot like her mom. I could never read her mom. She was a little more reserved than the moms I was used to. She carried herself like a lady at all times.

Those were my three main female friends and basically, they had been my whole life. They were all different from each other. Physically and mentally they each had different things to offer, that I loved.

This time around things were different. Sammy had been released from prison. He was about twenty years old now. Before we both were locked up, we had gotten really close, even though he was from Kinsman, he was genuine. The ultimate hustler. He rode his mountain bike everywhere. He wasn't the hardest guy but he was the smoothest and most determined kid I had ever met besides Raymone.

When I was released I wasn't hangin' out with Raymone so much anymore. The Crane boys had split up. Ced moved to Rawlings, down by Garden Valley with his cousin Germ. Vermaine migrated to 116th Street and Antonio had moved away somewhere and never came back to visit or anything. Larry and I started hangin' out a lot and even though he wasn't hustling he was always my favorite friend.

Sammy had gotten his teeth knocked out before he went to jail by some jack boys from over his way. He promised he'd have a mouth full of gold someday and he would never look back. He was aggressive with his words but sincere.

I hooked up with Tito as well. Tito was everything he said he was. When I called he provided me with weight. The Feds had picked up Gina. Ray C had shot at the police and got eight years and Nando had fell off miserably. He was smoking water fulltime and robbing everybody. A lot of new players in my age bracket had surfaced who wouldn't dare jump off the porch in 1990/1991. The game was wide open.

Bay-Bay had been killed, and ironically Suave had did a small bit and was back supplying the neighborhood. The hood had slowed down a little. I don't know if it was because the federal people had come and made Anderson a one-way street or was the crack game fading that fast. I jumped back in the game so fast it was like I never left. It felt second nature to me.

Cermaks had been shut down. All these years they were selling generic drugs in place of the real deal and getting top notch drug profits. It was all on the news. It was crazy 'cause I watched these men wear suits and ties every day and they were criminals, just like me.

Things started out slow. I went to John Adams. I was in the twelfth grade. I don't know how they put me there, but they did. I had a full schedule and classes with ninth and tenth graders. Mandatory Math and English classes that I needed in order to graduate. After about a week I had more desire for the streets than school so I stopped going completely. The new thing everybody was doing was smoking blunts and water and everybody was wearing braids. The movie, "Menace to Society" was out. Everybody wanted to be O-Dog, but not me.

Things had shifted. It seemed that everything had changed. Rob Pane, Reg and Blue were all ballin', as well as Marty, and that was fine. It was just funny because they were all getting high when I left.

Ray C and Gina had both been picked up and Nando wasn't doing as well. Things had shifted. New players had emerged. My team had switched to robbing the street corner hustlers. Every corner had at least ten guys standing on it, at all times. Carjacking's were at an all-time high as well. Everybody seemed to still be making money from selling crack, they were just alternating games.

I considered robbery a legitimate hustle. No crack meant go take. My whole entire block was doing it every night as soon as it got dark outside. The Gator Mask came out that year which was convenient. It had Velcro straps in the back and covered the bottom half of your face. I'm sure they were created for winter protection but for a robbery, it was perfect. They were sold on every corner at the Arab stores.

I quickly fell in line with the fellas. We would take turns driving and jumping out. We would split the money pretty much evenly all the way around. It was routine. Soon as it got dark we would posse up. Always At least three of us. The two who weren't driving would jump out before the car even stopped rolling, with the guns already raised. "DROP DOWN" we would yell and I can honestly say, if they ran, they rarely got away for many reasons. Sometimes they were chased down. Sometimes they were forced to stop, but they were always stopped. Raymone was so vicious he always shot you if you didn't have any money and sometimes when you did. You were doomed regardless.

If you ran, Tez would catch you for sure. I was the life saver. I would always spare them if they didn't have money. But I could usually talk them into giving everything up. I would say things like "Come on my nigga, it ain't worth your life. You can get back out here tomorrow and make more money. Be smart."

My crew didn't have any understanding or remorse. Sometimes we would shout out "Anderson Hustlers" after a robbery to let the other surrounding hustlers know we did it. It was a cake walk. Some nights we would split a few thousand. Sometimes we would watch their stashes before we hit them, but usually it was impulsive. We were ruthless. Times had really changed.

It felt good to finally be getting treated equal. I would sit up and really have to say to myself, "Damn niggas never try me anymore." I didn't know if it was because I had been to jail or if it was that I showed everyone I was willing to go the extra mile to get the money. Most of our block were robbers/hustlers, but the half who robbed; we never spoke about what happened the night before and if we did find a need to speak of it, we never mentioned it to the non-jackers.

I could tell that some guys still wanted to try me but they didn't. I was a lot bigger now and the thought of losing a fight to the Little Chris, that everyone use to bully, was probably their biggest fear. Then one day, Raymone and I had an argument about money. Not even a lot of money. Definitely, not enough to fall out over, in my opinion. There had already been boiling animosity between us, ever since I was released from jail. It felt almost like he couldn't accept me stepping out of his shadow. He would always say, "You ain't hard 'cause you been to jail." I would ignore him because I loved him like a big brother.

Thinking back, Raymone had always bullied me as much as everyone else. My grandmother always told me he wasn't my friend, but I couldn't see it. Then one day we were arguing over the phone and he told me he would come to my house and whoop my ass. I told him to come on over, but as soon as we hung up, immediate fear kicked in. I instantly felt like 'little ho ass Chris'. But remember, I'm shooting and robbing. I'd been to jail and had never truly lost a fight after twelve months of fighting much bigger tougher youth.

Then there was a loud banging at the door. I looked outside and it was Raymone kicking on my grandmother's door, loud. My granny had just paid $500 or $600 for her new security doors. And she loved that big white door. I instantly thought in my mind, "My granny has always stood up for me." I grabbed my 9mm. It was an ugly German Ruger I had bought from Brail Akbar, from Marah. It was ugly, but it was brand new. When I purchased it from him we shot it into the ground about ten times in broad day light. I gave him $150. Brail and I had always been close. Him and two of the other brothers, Sully and Rahid.

I went out the back door. The stairs to the front porch were on the side of the house so if you were on the porch, you couldn't view what was coming from the back yard.

When I appeared at the bottom of the steps, Raymone just looked down at me and said, "You gonna to shoot me?" I said, "I'm gonna kill you" and began to let off shots. He jumped over the porch banister and ran to his bike. I stopped firing, but when he was halfway up the street he began to talk smart and I shot at him once more. I really was hoping I didn't shoot him, but that started a feud between us for a few days.

We managed to not bump heads until about three days later in the playground, and everyone there knew that we were scheduled to fight or shoot on sight. I didn't have my gun on me and there was nowhere to go. Raymone was much taller than I was and about a year and some months older. I honestly couldn't imagine us fighting, but he talked so much and so loud about how "…he was eighteen years old and jail couldn't make me strong." I had to accept his challenge. Everyone in the neighborhood was there.

This was my first big fight in the hood, where it counted. Half of me wanted to run, the other half knew what I had been doing the last twelve months and wanted to test myself. Raymone was the same stature as Carlo Strong and I destroyed him and broken his nose so I thought, "What can I lose?" We began to fight. We slugged it out evenly at first until I figured out that I wasn't giving it my all. I turned the punch hard switch on, and like everyone else I had fought, I was way too hard of a puncher. I began to dominate the fight flawlessly. The longer we fought the easier it got. He backed up continuously talking and trying to amp himself up. We finally locked up and even in the wrestling department I was strong. I slammed him and they broke up the fight. He tried to shake my hand and I punched him again. The word was out. I had beaten Raymone. It didn't mean much. But it was Little Chris.

The days carried on. Fall had arrived. I still didn't have a steady girlfriend. I had started to hang out with Cordell a lot. He'd left Crane and began to hustle. He wasn't the smartest guy, but he was loyal and rode with me no matter what. I had been out on the streets about four months and gradually started to go back to just dealing crack. Cordell was my partner. We were like jelly and jam. Larry would come with us as well. But he refused to hustle.

Snoop Dogg came out that winter and even though The Chronic had been released the year before that was still the hottest tape besides Snoop Dogg. UGK's Pocket Full of Stones was hot and Mr. Big by 8Ball & MJG. The south and west had taken over music and we were actually still going to see Menace to Society at the theater. Selling crack was easy. So I felt all the way back in my element. But I always knew I could pick up the gun for that extra dollar. The fear you would see in a guy's eyes when he was looking down that barrel and when you mentioned the thought of his funeral they always went with the plan.

One day we were all standing on 99th and Union and Bolo walked up. Bolo was always theatrical seeming like he was up to something and if you were a stranger you would fear him, due to the way he talked and his look. He was cocky with a big mouth. Bolo had just been released from juvenile. When he approached the crowd he instantly began tapping some of the fellas' pockets asking, "What you got for me?" He tapped the pockets of about five guys' before he finally got to me. In the middle of his hand reach to my pocket, I grabbed his wrist and told him, "Ain't no nigga pocket checking me" and I pushed his hand back to him. He stepped back and looked at me and with the strongest, most intimidating voice he said, "Chris this Bolo," like I was supposed to acknowledge that fact and give him everything in my pockets. Then he looked down at my pockets like I was supposed to change my mind, realize I had made a mistake and empty my pockets.

Once we stared at each other for thirty seconds. I could tell he felt challenged and like he had to do something. Before I could react he punched me in my mouth. He punched me hard enough to fall back three or four feet into the wall of the apartment building we were standing by. When I bounced off the wall, before I could do anything I noticed my bottom tooth had went thru my lip. You could see the flesh. I ran into the Arab store. Cordell patched me up pretty good and asked me what I was going to do. I replied, "He put his hands on me".

Even though I was a little intimidated by Bolo, I was more upset. I was anxious to prove I was all that and could beat a big mouth. Everyone advised me to go home except Cordell. Most of the crowd was scared of Bolo and his brother Scoot. I had butterflies, but I knew I couldn't let that slide. I came out the store and before he could pep talk himself, the crowd was saying, "Aww shit, Chris and Bolo." Every car that was riding by seemed to know us and jumped out to watch the fight. We were both good basic boxers. But I used a textbook jab to keep him away until I was soon the aggressor. He was clearly no match. He continued to punch his fist together and yell, "Chris these hurt, especially in the winter," referring to his hands. It was a cold winter day outside and he was just backing up while promising me he would eventually knock me out. But it never happened. I had beaten somebody whose name meant something.

Cordell and I left. Scoot was there and even though Scoot was the toughest of all of us, Cordell promised that if Scoot did anything to help Bolo he would fight Scoot and from the looks of it, he was ready. Cordell was always ready.

15 In 1993, I learned that the game could change any second and that a man of no importance today, can be a man of great power tomorrow. Ced had moved to Rawlings. When we would play Rawlings in sports as kids, these boys had it harder than us. They were bums and looked dirty. In 1993, Hog, Germ, Red, Stomp, Joe-Joe and Lynn were all ballin'. They were all super clean with nice haircuts and cars. Vermaine's little brother Vernell was clean. He moved to Cedar with their dad, Ronald who had thirty children, literally.

A lot of new players had emerged; Dajuan Poe, Arch and Tim were from 116th and Greenwich. They were even riding motorcycles, and of course Bob from Superior was getting even more money. He was seventeen wearing gators with a Blazer and driving a Cadillac, but nobody hustled like Sammy. I knew all the major teenage players from any section close to me; Jock, Brick, Sherman and Tommy James. They were all from Prince. I'd known them all my entire life. Their crew was rumored to have hit a big lick. They all had luxury cars and they were all my age or two years older at the max. But Golden remained to reign supreme. He was the ultimate poster boy for what we all dreamed to be and Sammy was right on his heels.

Sammy would come and pick me up every other day to show me his new accomplishments. He was very secretive. He had apartments, way out. He had a kilo, a real fuckin kilo of coke. My boy Tito was my age and he was buying one as well. They both had real money. Bryan from my block was the only youth I had ever known to possess a kilo of cocaine, even though he might have robbed to get it.

He was the richest teen on 93rd and that was known and undisputed.

Sammy was about twenty years old and Golden was about twenty-one, but they were both young and gettin' it. Golden had a Corvette. He and Lil Tee both wore leather suits, Timberlands, and big jewelry. They had become larger than life. But I was more impressed by Jock from Prince. He ran Section Three and he was my age. He had a new Maxima.

From Garden Valley was Young Weirdo. These boys were all major players and I was thirsty to reach the same status. I knew it wasn't my time, but I continued to hustle.

My granny still worked and I still harbored all the teens cutting school. I hustled daily. I signed up at United Labor Agency on Lee road to get my GED. I was purchasing about 2 ounces of crack regularly, but I was actually still immature compared to the boys who were ballin'. I had a crazy hustle, but no saving habits. I bought Karl Kani and Girbruad with all my money or rented newer model dope fiend cars in order to seem or feel richer than I really was. I was maintaining $3000 to $5000, which was actually worse than I was doing before I went to jail at fifteen. But this year there was no Nando or Ray C to front me. I'm sure I could have found someone else but I had become content just knowing I had more than most, and my pager was jumpin'.

Christmas 1993, Cordell and I were riding in a fiend's 1993 Bonneville when the police got behind us. I took them on a high speed chase. We were going down Union, but as we past 93rd I began to speed up even though there was twenty inches of snow on the ground. When I got to

88th, I made a right and headed toward St. Catherine. Suddenly, the car sped out of control and we ran into a porch on the corner of St. Catherine. We jumped out of the car and took off, but we left behind a gun and about 100 rocks. It seemed like we were running for hours. When we finally made it back to Cordell's house, we took everything off and threw it down the laundry shoot, not knowing that the police had followed our footprints.

We got comfortable until we heard the knocks on the door. Cordell's mom let the police in. We were confident that we were scot free. The police began to ask questions and we denied everything. They went in the basement and matched our shoe sizes to our feet. We still denied everything until one officer asked Cordell, "If you guys have been in the house, how did you get snow all in your braids?" I looked over and sure enough there were thick patches of snow in Cordell's hair. I couldn't say another word. We both instantly shut up. We were cuffed and taken to jail.

Every hour they would try to convince me that Cordell had already ratted me out. But I had faith, until about five hours later when I saw Cordell walk silently past. He waved goodbye and he was released. I said and thought, "Damn, Cordell told." Then, in the middle of the night they called my name "Christian Hayward, juvenile." I thought they were going to transfer me from fourth district to the detention home, but I was met by Cordell's mom, Cordell, and my granny. Cordell was laughing, so I asked, "What happened?" and he said, "They kept trying to say that you told on me because you couldn't go back to jail." Cordell knew me, and he didn't believe them. Because we didn't say anything and you could only hold juveniles 24 hours without enough evidence, so they were forced to release us. Neither of us had said a word. Cordell was solid. So that was my Christmas 1993, not to mention that on my way to Cordell's house before the high speed chase, some guys jumped out and tried to rob me. I could have shot at them, but it all happened so fast. I ran up Beacon, jumped the fence and got away.

I brought in the New Year (1994) at Cordell's house at his moms New Year's party, shooting dice. I won about $4000 and swore that from then on, I would grind hard and save everything. I bought a new TEC-9 and a couple ounces of crack. A few days later, I was leaving the United Labor Agency and Cordell was taking all day picking me up, so I engaged in a dice game on Tarkington. Those boys up there were young and getting a lot of money. Getting the money right as the cars came off the freeway. That day the undercover police randomly hit their block. I didn't know anything about that neighborhood, so even if I wanted to run, I still would have gotten caught.

When the police ordered everyone to get up against the cars I told the officer I had a gun. They took it off my hip without conflict and put me in the car, but they missed the ounce of crack in my underwear. They never even checked me. I knew I was going to the detention home with no arguments. I sat at the fourth district for a few hours and then I was transferred to the detention home. I went with a gun charge. This time it wasn't new to me. They shipped me straight to 2B. The older repeat offender's dorm. The tougher guys were up there; Jerod McClare, Danny Alvin, Big Nose Boom, Nelly, Bernard and a few guys I knew from my previous juvenile bids. This time the teenage boys from across town were in there as well.

Bernard from Cliffview was there again and he was the leader of the Crosstown Boys. Most people knew Tamelli and Deli had money as well. They were from St. Clair. When they said they had Dayton rims and $20,000 cash, I just knew they were lying, but they had photos to prove it. These boys had hydraulics on their cars etc. But no matter what status anybody had from any side of town or section, most people liked me. I was cool with all the tougher guys and the guys that were rollin'. I talked shit with the niggas that I knew had more money than me, and I'd tell a nigga twice my size that if we got into a fight he would know I'd been there. I was seventeen now. My uncle had told me NO MATTER where I'm at to never show fear and ironically, he got out the weekend I got caught.

The detention home was a breeze this trip. A fight or two but nothing major. In February, I was sentenced to six months Ohio Department of Youth Services and they didn't count my detention home time because the judge said I was supposed to get a year for the gun charge. My uncle spoke at my sentencing, but they didn't care. Cuyahoga Hills School for Boys I went.

16

This time around was much different. As soon I hit the front door most people knew who I was, including the staff. I had the ultimate respect. Word travels fast. Everyone had a resume in jail. You're either respect worthy or not. There was no in between. The staff, Allen and Jafee remembered me. Allen and I shared the same birthday, August 12th. He was a silly and jolly older guy, with brown skin. Mr. Jafee was an older guy as well, really clean-cut, dark skin with a salt and pepper full beard. He was short and in good shape for his age. Allen and Jafee were opposite, but both cool.

My first day on orientation, I slapped a white boy and took the remote to the television and they moved me to my unit the next day. They moved me to A Dorm. It was the same as when I left. Just a new group of juveniles. A Dorm still wore blue. J DUB was the unit manager. Mr. Rope was our CO and Mr. Gray and a few other CO's, who's names I forgot. Cincinnati was still second runner up for the hardest crew after Cleveland. The leaders of this crew were Monkey Man and Darrick McKibb. Monkey Man was tall and dark and looked exactly like a monkey. Darrick was shorter than me, my complexion and sounded like he was from Texas. He had gold teeth and was on the wrestling team. He was so good they took him off campus to wrestle other high schools, etc. Monkey man was laid back. McKibb was loud and really silly. One time he knocked my dude Polo out with a body shot during a fight. The Nati boys were dogs, but we were tougher and we had more numbers.

My crew was Khalil Gro from EC, Andrell Mart from West 25th, Rell McRay and Hog from Rawlings. It was more of us than that. But those were the guys I was closest to. I knew all of them from the streets except for Khalil. He was a real cocky, black ugly kid with a loud mouth. Andrell Mart had a very deep voice and he was wide as a tank with super big lips. Hog was a little taller than me and dark skin. He was Rawlings' leader. I knew him my whole life because Ced would take us down to Rawlings to play them in sports. Hog had come up strong the first time I got locked up, before that he was the dirtiest of them all. Oh, and I forgot this kid from 131st, Darnell Jackson aka D-Rock. He was a real nice looking kid but very, very violent. When he wasn't violent he was mild mannered. He had a sinister laugh and everyone knew he meant business. He was a year younger than me but a little taller and he reminded me of Muhammad Ali. In his mind, no man could beat him in anything. He wore a size thirteen shoe and his hands were about a foot long and I'm not exaggerating. Darnell and I were closer than anybody.

Our crew was pretty tight, except the fact that Andrell didn't like Rell. But I would keep the peace. Rell was a bully. He was about 6' tall and nicely built. I knew Rell my whole life because his grandmother Ms. Gapp lived three houses up from me. We were the first two black families on Gibson.

One day on our way to recreation, Rell stepped out of line and they punished the whole pod by not letting us go play basketball. When the staff asked, "Does anybody have a problem with not being able to go to recreation, it was silent. Nobody would dare say anything against Rell. Thinking that we were all on the same team Rell loudly spoke out, "Nobody bet not say shit!" and before I could blink, Andrell had stepped out of the line and spoke loudly, "Bitch I like basketball." The whole pod was shocked, but you could tell they were happy.

Rell was a menace and the pod bully. I was caught in the middle, but I could look in Andrell's eyes and see that I couldn't stop him. When we got back to the unit, Rell kept giving me the puppy dog look like he wanted me to stop Andrell. But I couldn't. I honestly didn't think Andrell could beat Rell, but Rell was scared to fight and it was clear to everyone. Rell put his hands up, out of fear. They were two gigantic teenagers, so it was an even fight. Andrell's first two blows knocked Rell silly. Rell backed up as Andrell kept swinging very hard punches. He hit Rell in the eye and what happened after that was history. I had seen guys back up before. I had even seen guys get dropped, but never had I seen one of my guys turn around completely and take off running. Rell grabbed his eye and ran out the unit hollering. I was embarrassed for him. Andrell had given Rell new status. Nobody respected Rell again, not even the white boys. Rell's eye was black for months it seemed. It was terrible. Andrell told me afterward that he knew Rell was soft and he hated him since the day I introduced them. Andrell like myself hated big mouth bullies.

Now that my Uncle Tug was out, I received a visit every Saturday like clockwork. He would sneak me a $20 bill and I would get street food and candy all week long. I was living pretty well. He would bring my friends, girlfriends, etc., to visit me. He made my bid pass quickly. He even beat up an older guy in the neighborhood who had once pulled a gun on me after a fist fight. I was seventeen and he was about twenty-four or twenty-five when we fought. He couldn't except that I was winning the fight and he ran and got a gun. That happened right before I got locked up. Tug heard about it when he got out and during one of his visits, he asked me why I didn't tell him. When I confirmed it, he put the guy in the hospital. Everyone in the neighborhood agreed it was a bloody massacre. My granny was mad because Tug was still on parole.

This juvenile stretch was much easier than the last. But I complained even more. I never thought about getting a job no matter how much preaching Tug did. Tug was my father, my friend and my brother. We laughed the whole visit. Even though he was only thirty-two, to me, that was old. He was still beating guys up and selling crack. I would think, "He's too old for that shit," but in reality he was still very young.

One day after a visit we were watching a movie and the remote to the TV was only held by the top dogs. This day, I had the remote and the Cincinnati boys said they were supposed to have it. So of course, their front man Darrick McKibb stepped up. He said, "Hayward y'all been had the remote too long." I replied by letting him know I wasn't giving it up. He said if I didn't give him the remote he was going to get his shoes. I told him to go get them and I started to get up, but when I did Darrick pushed me back down on the couch. He stood over me so I couldn't get up. The crowd went wild. They knew it would be Hayward vs McKibb.

I was cool with Raymond Tall from the Nati from my first juvenile bid and he would tell them I was no joke. He tried to break it up. But Darrick had pushed me. There was no turning back. I was very nervous, but this was the moment everyone had been waiting on including the staff. The staff actually got on the phone and called other staff from other units saying, "Hayward and McKibb are about to fight." Before McKibb came back from getting his shoes everyone had moved the furniture and the day room was set up like a pit for two fighters. All I could hear was the Nati boys saying, "Slam him," and Khalil Gro yelling, "That's Chris Haywarth (pronounced wrong in his southern accent). Y'all got the land fucked up!" McKibb arrived from the back of the dorm, and got directly into his wrestling stance and I got into my textbook boxing stance and instantly we began to rumble.

We slugged hard but I was getting more punches in. I managed to avoid the slam until after missing a right hand, Darrick did manage to grab and slam me. I locked his arms so he couldn't punch and everyone broke up the fight. We jumped up and squared off again. I jabbed while Darrick waited on the perfect moment to get the slam. It was strategic. We battled like two warriors and he actually punched pretty hard. He ended up slamming me again. This time his arms were lose and we were punching each other even with me lying on my back until they broke it up. We both got up out of breath. I respected him and I could see he respected me, but we still went at it again. Slugging slow and hard toe to toe and blow for blow until we locked up and McKibb slammed me again. This time so hard, that snot was all over my face. I felt all the wind come out of my body. I was done. But this time he didn't try to punch. He just laid on top of me until they broke it up. The whole pod began to clap loudly. It was probably the best fight they had ever seen. It was the best, but hardest fight I had ever been in. The next day, I was playing spades and McKibb tapped me on the shoulder. I was thinking, "God please don't let him say he wants to fight again." But instead he said, "I respect you Cleveland," and I shook my head and told him I felt the same. From then on, it was a mutual respect between us.

Soon afterwards, A Dorm became routine. I had received my GED and I had two months to go. I was moved to H Dorm with Big Nose Boom, Mickey from DTW, Party Arty from St. Clair, and my little dude from the hood, Silver.

H DORM was all the way on the other side of the institution, the worst dorm on that end. They wore maroon or gold. I was good anywhere I went. I had my respect. When you were a dog you automatically fit in with the dogs. H Dorm was a little more laid back than A Dorm.

My bunky was a guy name Rylin from Detroit. He was really tall with all gold teeth. He had long red dreadlocks and he was light skin. His whole style was different than ours. All he talked about was himself and his older brothers and cousins being rich in Detroit, and how much more advanced he was than us. He said that when he came to Ohio, he caught a bad break. He also mentioned that he might be picked up for some murders back in Detroit. I thought everything he said was a lie. To me, he had a big mouth, but at times he was cool.

My visits were the same. My uncle never missed. He would always preach about me getting out and getting a city job, or boxing seriously. He would always say, "When you get older boxers will be getting $50 million a fight." I'm laughin' to myself and thinking', "This nigga crazy." Crack was king to me and my mind was already made up. He would always tell me how my crew wasn't doing anything and they were not as advanced as me and I needed to branch out. We laughed our entire visit.

Nothing about my uncle had changed, since I was a baby. He talked, walked and laughed at the same. He always kept it real and never sugar coated anything. He gave me the pros and cons. Even though I'm sure he wanted better for me. I could tell he was happy I was considered a dog in and out of jail and not soft. He would tell me stories about his old running buddies in the 70s and early 80s. All his stories were raw. I always felt genuine love from him. He hadn't started back using drugs. He was actually doing well and I was happy. He had a new Cadillac and was consistently in the gym. He always preached how important working out was even if it was just a small amount daily.

Back on the unit, I would talk to Cee-Cee every day on the phone. We had planned to be together when I got out. I had about sixty days left. I was scheduled to leave in August right before I turned eighteen. I was grown this time around, so I didn't have to listen to anyone. I could hustle all night. This would be the time.

One night while I was trying to sleep, my bunky (Rylin) was masturbating and it was vibrating the bed. He would do this often and actually it was a violation every time he did it, but I minded my business and ignored the vibration of the bed. But this particular day, I was fed up so I asked him to go to the bathroom and he refused. People in the surrounding bed areas began to laugh as Rylin put the cover back over his head and began to masturbate even harder. So the vibration moved violently until he was done. I was embarrassed and I felt disrespected. The unit was quiet. I had made up my mind that the next day I would confront Rylin and force him to back up all the Detroit talk.

I didn't speak to Rylin all the next day, but when second shift came in if you had a problem with another youth they would usually tell the unit to form a circle and pick out your opponent. For that to happen, the staff person, Mr. Angeles had to be there and today he was. When shift changed we formed the circle. Before they could ask who had problems I stepped in the circle. When Angeles asked me who I wanted to fight I pointed to Rylin. Everyone was in disbelief and most people wanted to see Rylin take that fall. He acted like he really didn't want to fight, but he had to.

The case managers were Ms. Apple and Ms. Adam. They both aided me with getting into A Dorm, so I kinda felt bad, but this had to be done. As soon as Rylin put his hands up I began to knock him around like a punching bag. He was no match. Even with his height he was no factor. His last option was to grab me. I even man handled him then. Everyone was laughing at him. Fighting him was like fighting a girl. When they broke the fight up I made him aware that if he masturbated again, I would beat him up and strip him totally naked. He never did it again during his last week In Cuyahoga Hills.

The next week he was extradited back to Detroit for murder. It was sad. We all felt bad as he walked out shackled. He looked like he wanted to cry. He had on Patton leather red high top Adidas and a fly ass jogging suit. I never found out what happened to him. I just know I didn't want his position. A few weeks later I went home.

17

It was a hot summer day in August. Tug picked me up in his Cadillac, but his demeanor was different. All he talked about is me not worrying his mom and me not selling drugs and hanging with the same people. All that shit went in one ear and quickly out the other. I had a plan.

When I got home my granny was happy to see me. She acted like she had a secret that only she knew. When Tug left we talked on the porch for hours. Granny rarely came to see me, but it was cool. She came with my Aunt Gale when they could. After talking granny took me in the house and handed me an envelope. She had resigned from working. But she told me she saved me some money. She didn't know I had a stash from when I left. She proudly handed me $1,500 and said, "This should be enough for you to not sell drugs and get a job." Of course, I said yes. But in my mind granny had just boosted the package fair. The first thing I bought was a pager. I would be eighteen years old in a week. You couldn't tell me nothing. Cee-Cee and I proceeded as a couple like we said we would. It was 1994. The world was mine.

The day after I got out Tug took me to visit the new county jail they were just finishing up. He told me I would be there soon if I started back doing the same things. He told me how he and Gale had already scheduled for me to fill out an application with the city, as a waste collector. Tug was on my back, hard. I would say, "Tug, I'm grown," and he would say, "No, you're not. You're almost an eighteen year old child." When my eighteenth birthday came, Tug took me to take the test for my temporary driver's license. I failed the test. Then, he preached to me the importance of patience and being prepared. He was beginning to be a pest. Every day I hustled hard. I hustled until I comfortably was able to buy an eighth of a key. That would cost me anywhere between $2800 and $3200, depending on if you bought it hard or soft or who you bought it from. By then, Sammy and Tito were on, so I never had to branch out. They were both my close friends, so I could get the work from them.

Although I hustled daily, I still filled out the application for the city job. I had only been out of jail thirty days and I had already bought me a Regal and put Seven Stars on it. It was real clean. It was nice. My granny was pissed and Tug took my car keys until I received my license. No matter how grown I was, as long as I was living under my granny's roof, she and Tug were both always breathing down my back.

I would go to Dove playground or over on Matilda sometimes because they had the big crap games. But on Matilda they also had Lori, the finest girl up that way. She was a little older than me and she had a brother name Londo. I don't think he was too fond of me, but I wanted Lori. She had an older boyfriend with a lot of money and he was clearly out my league and much bigger than I was, but that didn't stop me from looking.

One day, while leaving Matilda, Lori flagged me down. I stopped and we began to talk. She began telling me how cute I was. I was nervous and asked her about her boyfriend. She replied, "What about him?" She asked me to come back at midnight. I couldn't wait. I pulled in the driveway and knocked on the door and to my surprise Londo answered. I felt like I had gotten over when he said "What u want?" He was implying that I shouldn't be at his house for any reason. I stuck my chest out and said, "Lori." He looked at me with a mad look and shut the door. A second later Lori arrived. She had a big Kool-Aid smile. We sat on the front porch and actually laughed and had great conversation.

I was actually waiting on her dude's car to come pulling up but he never did. Then about 2 am she said the most shocking thing to me, "Pull yo dick out". I was taken by surprise. But I did it, and as soon as I did she grabbed it with both hands and began to caress it. Right outside on her front porch. She told me I was holding and she led me too her basement. I hadn't had many sexual experiences due to me being in jail. So I wanted to perform up to parr. Lori didn't waste any time. She made we aware that her dad and brother could hear her if she was too loud. She put the condom on me and got on top of me. She rode me really, really well. She knew what she was doing. Not like the other teenage girls before her. I left feeling like I had won in two ways.

Londo knew I fucked his sister and it was always a stripe to fuck a queen from another section. The Lori thing was short lived. The third time I snuck over there I was in the basement and Lori came downstairs and said, "Some man is at my door asking for you." It was about 1 am. So I went upstairs to see Tug at the side door telling me it was too late for me to be outside. The "Man I'm grown" line meant nothing. I was embarrassed to the max. I never called Lori again. He would always embarrass me and then tell me the reason why. Then he would tell me that he loved me. His main reason for coming to get me from Lori's that night was because I had to get up early to see my PO.

The next morning we trailed each other downtown. Tug and granny rode together and me by myself. We all entered the state building together and went up to the parole officer's office. The PO began explaining that I would have to get a job and report once a month, etc. In mid conversation I stood up and said, "I'm grown. I'm not reporting to you at all. I'm not a juvenile anymore," and I walked out. As I walked to the elevator, Tug said, "Chris you gone disrespect mom like that by just walking out" and I replied, "I'm not disrespecting mom, but I'm grown, I'm not doing no parole." I jumped on the elevator alone.

I'm not sure what floor we were on but when I got to the main lobby, Tug was waiting at the elevator door when it opened. There were about 200 people watching as he shouted, "You think you grown?"

Before I could reply I felt the hardest punch I had ever felt. I don't remember falling. I just remember laying on my back dazed. As I got up, I could see Tug there with his hands up in his stance. A perfect stance. I was upset. I had never ever been dropped. I had never knew punches could feel that way but I still charged him like a bull and some way he managed to move to the side and hit me two more times even harder. I had spank many asses, but this was a whole different animal. I couldn't see or feel my body. All I could do was retreat. It felt like every bit of manhood I had, was stepped on. I ran as fast as I could past all the people in the lobby. That run seemed like a mile of shame run. I ran all the way to tower city parking and sat in my car for an hour. My ego was crushed. I didn't go home for days. I hustled for three days nonstop.

I got the job with the city and everybody was happy. I was even happy, although I had gotten caught with nineteen rocks and $300 the week before. My first adult case. Tito bonded me out because Tug told mom to leave me in jail to see what it was like. My granny always held my money or knew where it was.

When I was released from the county, I started my new job. My first day, I was assigned to the 55th station where my Aunt Gale had the juice. I was on the garbage truck with a kid name Chad Black, Jr. He was very young as well, but not as young as me. He was about twenty-three years old. A nice looking, tall, slim kid. He was light skin with curly hair and he was always talking 'bout making it big as a rapper, but his skills didn't seem too promising.

The driver was Marv Deuce, a big, brown skin, country nigga with a killer smile. Marv, Chad, and I were the perfect team. Chad cursed out policemen, the foreman, and co-workers and he smoked weed on the truck and beat up pedestrians. Chad was young and didn't give a fuck about nothing and nobody. Chad even killed rats when they jumped out the truck. He was fearless. He was my boy. As far as Chad was concerned, everybody was a bitch or a ho. His father, Chad Black, Sr., was a big time bondsman and his mother, Sarah, was a big time insurance agent. Chad's ego was too big to deal with his father. Big Deuce was the driver, but some days when we were behind schedule, he would jump out and help finish the route.

I threw garbage in the daytime and I would hustle until 7 pm before going to Cee-Cee's house. Her mom, Selina, would tell everybody that came over, "Cee-Cee got a city working man, making good money." I guess that was good, considering Cee-Cee was only sixteen and I was eighteen. Cee-Cee and I had sex every day in every position. We were daredevils. Selina talked on the phone 24 hours and she was so loud, we always knew when she was coming.

Cee-Cee had a little cousin Nini, that Selina had adopted, and a bad ass little sister. The house was full of estrogen. I loved Cee-Cee. We experimented with everything we could, sexually. Oral sex was off limits to most teens but not to us. We had sex in every room in the house. It was amazing. Selina cooked almost every day and although sometimes she was a real bitch, she treated me like a son. Selina also liked my Uncle Tug. Sometimes they would get on the phone and reminisce about John Adams High School days.

Winter was approaching. My Regal had been stolen, so I would alternate using my uncle's Cadi or my aunt's brand new red Cutlass. My aunt let me use her car to go to Adams' Homecoming Dance. Me, Larry, and Elmar decided to go to the mall before the dance. The Jordan's, were released that weekend. The ones with Michael Jordan's accomplishments written on the bottom of the shoe. I bragged all day about having $6000 in my pocket while driving my aunt's brand new car. I was untouchable. We were leaving the mall and stopped in JC Penny. I asked Elmar, "You think they'll notice if I steal this thermal shirt?" Larry said (always being the logical thinker), "Chris you got thousands on you. Just buy the thermal."

I had robbed and done everything violent under the sun, but never shoplifted anything outside of candy from Pick-N-Pay. So, I walked out with the blue thermal, polo shirt. We made it all the way to the front door. I thought I had won until two plain clothes gentlemen walked up and asked me to look in my bag. I said, "Hell naw," then I changed it around and said, "Okay, I'll pay y'all." They said, "You can't pay us, they want you downstairs." They cuffed me. All I could think about was missing that dance and not being able to show off in my aunt's car. They walked me through the whole mall. I was so ashamed looking like a million dollars going down for theft. They gave me a $1000 bond and surprisingly my aunt picked me up and still let me use her car.

We went to the dance clean as ever. My girl Cee-Cee went to South High. But I was dating some of the finest chicks at John Adams as well. That was my neighborhood school. The female I was focused on, I'll call her Ms. B. She was attractive and a lot of the guys wanted her. I think she was dating one of my homeboys. But I wasn't sure. At this time in my life it seemed like I had super powers over the girls and I loved it.

Ms. B and I left the dance early. We drove around talking and laughing listening to "Drifting on a memory, ooh ooh ooh, ain't no place I rather be than with you," all night. We finally stopped at Nathan Hale Jr. High School parking lot and began to kiss. As we kissed she did this thing with her tongue and she licked all over my face violently, while moaning. I had never been so turned on to turn somebody on. Spit was everywhere and I loved it. Ms. B had on a leather skirt and some lace stockings. She had a million dollar walk, dark brown skin with a smile that nobody could match. When Ms. B took her panties off my aunt's whole car began to smell like I had opened a can of sardines and poured it all over. The windows were very foggy. I couldn't believe or adjust to the smell. I quickly put my dick back in my black Nautica corduroys and gave her a reason I had to go. I was so disappointed. Her thighs were dripping wet. Her whole bottom half, but the smell was unbearable. I dropped her off at home on Kinsman and went home. My night was ruined.

18

That year the guys in my crew that were booming was Boo-Baby, Bryan (as always), Tez and myself. Boo-Baby had a Cougar on gold Dayton's. I had a lime green Malibu and Bryan and Tez both had multiple cars. The Bonneville boys, Ali and Buddy, had emerged as well. They were first cousins and they looked alike, both were brown skin, but Buddy was nice looking and Ali was real ugly. Ali was very muscular and Buddy was medium build. Buddy was from the neighborhood. He was three years younger than me, but we were always cool. He had mad hustle. Ali was two years younger than me, and he had even more hustle. Buddy was laid back. Ali was a live wire. He was a ruthless young cat who had lost both his parents and grew up in foster homes. He was a decent fighter and a better shooter. He and Buddy had the weirdest bond. They both had the biggest block heads. They were either my height or an inch taller. Ali and I never got along. We were comrades due to being from the same neighborhood, but that's about it. I think he always wanted to try me. He wasn't soft but he knew he was no match for me.

The Bonneville boy's grandfather lived on the corner of Anderson, smack dab in the middle of the action. When we were little he would pour oil on all the bricks that we sat on while hustling to keep us away, but it never worked.

That winter, the Anderson Hustler's stayed at war with a lot of the surrounding neighborhoods, particularly Union and 108th. Those on 108th were strong, but Union was not. Union consisted of everybody from 103rd to the boulevard.

They had us outnumbered, but we were known for fighting hard, sticking together and shooting faster.

In 1995, when the New Year came in, I was working, hustling, and fighting a small drug and petty theft case. I brought the year in with Cee-Cee riding me on the couch. I thought she was the finest chick in the world. She was in cosmetology school at South High and all the popular chicks hated her.

Ironically, my friend Kimmie lived on the same street as Cee-Cee and Cee-Cee was always jealous of me and Kimmie's relationship. Even though I had taken Kimmie's virginity, the sex never affected our friendship. I loved Kimmie on a whole different level. I had known her since I was a child. Sometimes, when I fell off I could call her to give me money to re-up. Just a double up for $40 or $50, to get back on my feet. If I was stranded she would come as well. Kimmie had a boyfriend who didn't understand our bond, nor could any of the females that I became involved with understood, but they had to deal with it. She was one of my dearest friends. We grew up with the same struggles. I could talk to her about anything. I could tell her my deepest and darkest secrets without being judged or feeling ashamed. I could be myself.

I spent New Year's Day at Cee-Cee's house. The next day I was scheduled to work and get back on my normal program. Sometimes, Cee-Cee had a way of making me forget to hustle for days. I called my friend Martin to pick me up. Martin and Larry, arrived about 1 am on January 3rd, in a brand spanking new car. Also, riding in the car were Roc and Martin's younger brother, Darrick. They were both

Crab's sons. We were like cousins. The car was packed but I had license, so I drove. I failed to ask where they'd got the car.

When we got to 93rd, one street from my house a car full of grown men, cut us off and one guy jumped out and ran towards us screaming, "Get the fuck out my car!" Then, the whole car full of men jumped out. They rushed the driver's door and said, "Man, I got car jacked for this car!" So I'm stuck. The only thing I could think to do was pull out my gun and say "back up" and they all did as we began to get out the car. While we were getting out somebody had already called the police. They were approaching from everywhere. We all took off and I ran with Larry and as he jumped the fence the police were right behind us. All that kept playing in my mind was my Uncle Tug saying, "Always run your own way." I ran to the right and I was met by two police cars, so I ran off of Crane back towards 93rd and Benham, all the time forgetting the fact that I had a loaded 357 on me and four and a half ounces of freshly cut crack.

I ran up Benham and when I thought the police weren't looking, I threw the weapon along with the drugs. I was surrounded by the time I reached 96th and Benham. There were literally ten cars. It was over. They cuffed me and put me in the car. Then one cop showed up holding the two large bags of crack and another one holding the gun. I was doomed, sitting in the back seat arguing that neither were mine. Then they brought a lady and a guy to my window and asked them was I the guy who carjacked them and unbelievably, they said, "Yes. By that time all the actual carjackers were caught as well. They asked me if these guys were with me, and I said, "No." They said you're going down all by yourself. I just took the charges and went to County Jail. The next day I was placed in the misdemeanor bullpen and I couldn't believe it. I had only been charged with name falsification and released on a personal bond. I had beat the system. It was sweet!

I stayed out of jail all of January and February. I was scheduled for sentencing at the end of February for the drug case, which had been dropped to drug abuse. My boy, Ike from the School of Science had a son born earlier that month, so we celebrated. He was doing pretty well. Tez and I had started hitting licks again. Anderson was Anderson. The block was wild. My uncle was back getting high and robbing everybody. I was just waiting to be sentenced, saving my money and paying my lawyer. My aunt resigned me from the city of Cleveland, Waste Collection, so I could get my job back when I completed my sentence.

I sold my Malibu and bought a 1987 maroon Cutlass. The big day came and I went to sentencing. My lawyer said that "something" had popped up and that I had big issues. I said, "there has to be a mistake." Then, he pulled out an indictment for armed robbery, drug trafficking, and CCW. I almost fainted. I had been indicted for the previous cases from January 3rd while leaving Cee-Cee's house. He said the judge was willing to resolve all these matters today and that my sentence could be very lenient, if I told who was with me. Even though I was scared, I knew that telling wasn't an option. I asked my lawyer, "How much time?" and he explained, "two to ten." I yelled, "Hell Naw!" and started crying. I asked could I go home and come back and I was permitted to do so.

I went and got my uncle. He was skinny as hell and looking his worst, but he came to court. Me, him, and Larry. Tug coached me all the way through by saying, "Whatever you do, get flat time. No tail". I told the lawyer that and he left and came back and said, "The judge said six flat." I cried even harder. He explained that six was four and I would be out at age twenty-two. I said, "Fuck that!"

My uncle said, "Take that shit," so, I agreed to six years like an asshole. When I went in front of the judge he gave me a break. He surprisingly sentenced me to four years in Lorain Correctional and my lawyer advised me that I would do exactly three and be out at twenty-one years old. I was cuffed and remanded to county jail. I cried until the day I left county. It was all like an unbelievable movie. That day in the county jail, I met Pete. He was four years older than me and he was a lot smaller and skinnier than I was, but everyone respected him. We were both sentenced and going to the tenth floor. I had only heard stories about the tenth floor and I was wondering why the fuck I was going there. I was only eighteen and had never been to county. I told Pete that I was nervous. He was loud, wild, reckless, and didn't give a shit about nothing. He saw that I was nervous and promised me that if I had a problem he would be back to back with me. To the tenth floor, 10A we went.

Everybody in our pod was twenty-one or older and every single person on the pod had a murder case. I saw Peanut and Spikey from juvenile. They both had murders. Super-Jay Jerod had robbed a jewelry store and had been shot up really bad in the process. I had three years and these guys were getting life.

G Murder from 71st, Wink, Jacus Rollins aka J-akus and Crick and Big Tone from EC and Jason from the Westside and Dennis came from St. Clair. That pod was real. Everybody gambled all day long. They called me Shorty 'cause I was so little, but I was cool. And I can't forget Gary. He was from Cedar along with Pete. Gary killed someone outside Club Ninety-One. The tenth floor was the dungeon. They locked us in without any real supervision. The tough talk was no good up there AT ALL!

J-akus beat his murder case. G murder beat his murder case and Q from the projects beat his as well. Wink and Gary weren't so lucky. William Spence, a guy that I had known from juvenile, came back from prison for an early release and had gotten turned down.

What I noticed early was that juvenile just groomed young youth for prison because traveling the county jail hallways, I'd seen all the guys that I had been locked up with in the different juvenile facilities. It was like we all just graduated to another level of being criminals.

I was finally shipped to Lorain, which turned out to be reception for all the prisons up North. It looked like a gigantic college campus. It wasn't like juvenile. There were thousands of inmates. As soon as you got there you received your number, all your hair was removed from your face and head and you were issued a jump suit. Going through Lorain was degrading. Thirty men at a time, standing butt ass naked in a circle on some pre-carved footprints waiting to receive instructions from a guard to bend over and open our asshole and cough, etc. Basically, stand with a bunch of naked ass niggas in the cold for fifteen minutes and wait to get violated. Those type of moments make you start to think twice about the life you had chosen. But you quickly snap out of it when you and the fellas get together and talk the street shit.

My first celly in Lorain was Poo Harold from East Cleveland. He was an older cat around thirty-five years old. He was light skin with big lips, real clean cut. Everybody knew Poo Harold. I guess where he was from, he was somebody. In the cell he was silly and laid back. We had a lot of fun. He schooled me to the ways of the joint. My running buddies were Lil Rick, Mont and Alvin Newell. I adjusted. I would rob cells for commissary with my boys and talk to Poo all night. He always cracked jokes on me because I slept in my one piece jumper. He called me, "Ready to roll." Poo schooled me about doing time, as well as, women while doing time and how you couldn't worry about what they were doing on the outs.

I met another older guy name Box, from 105. He was about fifty. Box was a short real wide, ugly man. He would brag that he couldn't read a lick but he could count. Box was wealthy from dealing heroine. He always told me don't ever try drugs and I would be cool. Even though I wasn't good at Spades, he always made me his partner and taught me to play. We played Chess as well, and he always stressed the fact that math was associated with everything. Maybe that was his way of deflecting from the fact that he couldn't read, but he was right on a lot of levels.

My day was balanced. I was cool in the cell with Poo. I was cool on the floor with Box. The floor had all bunk beds, lined up. It seemed like thousands of them. The rest of the pod was made up of two levels of cells. I walked to eat with my boys. Alvin Newell was a tall, athletic built kid from West 25th. He was brown skin and always smiled. Mont was also from West 25th. He was short and real dark. Mont was a funny looking character with an attitude to match. I had known Mont since kindergarten at Hicks Montessori School, but we hadn't seen one another since third grade. Nonetheless, I knew who he was as soon as I saw him and vice versa. Mont actually introduced me and Alvin.

Rick was a stick-up kid from my side of town. He was shorter than I was, stocky and brown skin, with a low voice and a very mild attitude. However, when you pissed him off, he was ready. We were all eighteen years old, all had two to four years, and all hoped we would get super-shocked or some type of early release. We also, all hoped that we would ride out together and be sent to the same parent institution. But all that those hopes were short lived when Alvin hit this big white guy and the guy had a seizure. We were all split up and moved. Alvin hit him so hard they thought we jumped him. We were all separated and moved to different pods.

While I was being escorted to my new pod this Asian sergeant (I forget his name, but I do remember that everyone hated him) continued to aggravate me by explaining to me that I was being put in a cell with somebody I wouldn't want to be with. I was 'Lil Chris' I could get along with anybody. Then we entered the pod and I was directed to my cell. It was an upstairs corner cell. When the cell door opened and I looked in, I saw a homosexual. But not an ordinary homosexual. It was a homosexual name "Mack Momma" from Akron. This guy considered himself to be a real woman, but he was built up like a football player. The rumor was that this guy could play basketball, football and fight. I can't lie, I was uncomfortable. I walked in the cell trying to maintain my, "I don't take no shit" aura. He said, "What's up?" and gave me its name. He didn't refer to himself as Mack Momma just yet.

EAZY-E died and O.J. Simpson beat his murder trial that year. History was being made. O.J., Eazy E and now me in a cell with this guy. The only way to get out of the situation was to check-in and only suckas crashed out or checked in. We began to talk. He began telling me about his life and that he was from Akron and had a twin brother. He explained to me for days how he robbed banks. He said he only drove BMWs and even though he seemed to live a great life on the streets he still seemed right at home in the cell. Every morning he woke up, burned a match and proceeded to wet the match and use it as eyeliner then put on a bunch of Vaseline. He told me that his brother wasn't gay, but they use to have orgies on the weekend with the older neighbors and that's how he was turned out. The brother participated in the orgies but never took the homosexual route, once the phase was over.

The penitentiary was a whole different experience for me. You could spend $25 a week in reception, but that $25 seem to go a very long way. I had been in the cell with the guy for about a week and everything was fine until one night while we were talking and he asked me a shocking question. He said, "If I sucked your dick would that make you gay?" I said, "If a man touches my leg, I'm gay. "So he proceeded on and on trying to convince me to have sex with him.

This was the first time I felt really challenged in years. This guy was twice my size and knew how to do time. His voice had gotten more aggressive as he finally challenged me to either do as he said or leave the cell. I hadn't coward to any human being in years, and even though I was scared to death I still felt my right hand wouldn't fail. I took that deep breath as I stood with my back against the cell window bars and told the guy, "We gotta do what we gotta do. I'm not gay." I could have made a scene and gotten removed from the cell, but I didn't know what the story might have been once it got out. Me and him locked eyes and just stood there. That moment I realized I was still a little boy. Because two guys with that homosexual mindset could have easily taken advantage of me. He sat down and began to take deep breaths insinuating he was upset. I kept my position against the bars. Many thoughts going thru my head. But the main one was, "I just need to make it through tonight and I'll figure out a plan B."

I didn't go to back to sleep. I sat up on my bed until breakfast. I proceeded to breakfast like nothing happen. When I got back from breakfast, he apologized, but in my mind I knew the only thing that was stopping me from beating this guy all the way up was the size difference and fear of the unknown. I was boiling inside. However, I knew that if I ever saw Mack Momma again and I had the ups, I would beat him up.

I never really spoke to the homosexual again. Actually, three or four days later I was transferred. I opened up a new minimum security penitentiary, Richland Correctional Institution (RiCI). It was the minimum camp connected to the walls which was Mansfield, the most notorious jail in Ohio, besides the Southern Ohio Correctional Facility (SOCF) aka Lucasville, which was famous for the Lucasville riots, multiple jail murders and rapes. It stayed on the news. It was like an old tale that older guys talked about, unbelievable to a youth.

Mansfield was close security and rumored to be equally as violent, but I was minimum security so I didn't have to worry about ever seeing either. The bus ride to RiCI was wild. I met a lot of guys from all over the City of Cleveland and most of us were between the age of eighteen and twenty. Everybody was wild and ready. When the bus load was dropped off we were met by an older crew of inmates between the ages of twenty-one and twenty-five who had been transferred from J Dorm due to it being about to close. There weren't a lot of older guys in RiCI.

We wore tan, khaki suits. This was nothing like the movies with the blue and sky blue suits. This was sweet and unorganized. RiCI was so fresh, that they didn't even have many rules. I knew half of the faces from juvenile and everyone I knew respected me. I was one of the guys you automatically knew to respect. My crew was Big Art Lepp from 131st, Devin Cones from Tarkington, Chicago Mone from St. Clair, Tyler from Hough, Quinn and Puerto Rican Dave were both from the Westside. All Dave did was talk about his girl but I knew him from juvenile from hanging with Dreco and Lil P. They were all Puerto Ricans who were also the first juveniles I ever heard of that sold heroine and made a lot of cash.

Boo Mack from Bartlett was about twenty-one or twenty-two years old, a very reserved guy. He was tall, lanky, and dark skin with a round head and a perfect smile. His physical appearance didn't fit his reputation. I had never seen him before now. I had only heard stories. He was supposed to be this ruthless, killer jack boy, but all he did was smile and brush his waves all day. We would talk, laugh and crack jokes. He didn't hang around my crew. I also hung with the older crew, Tune from 105. Nick B from Lakeview, Booch from Miles, and Mack Blarock. All these guys were at least twenty-four or twenty five and they all called me Shorty. They seemed really old to me.

My crew, we called ourselves the Big Timers. We all got clothes and food boxes in, every week or two. We all wore Jordan's and Air Max. Chicago Mone wore diamonds and gold. We all talked about how much money we had, how many cars we had, and how many chicks we fucked. Jail was a big competition and fashion show. We played football against all the older J Dorm boys. They all stuck together and so did we. The rec yard was directly in the middle of the two big dorms. We all shared the basketball court and weights.

Time flew by in RICI. My crew was young boys. We all thought we were tough, except Devin. He was just a real nice looking kid, a player, from Tarkington. He was tall and dark skin. All he and I did was listen to 8Ball & MJG's, "On Top of the World tape," and argue about who was better between 2Pac, Scarface, Michael Jordan and Magic Johnson.

I loved Devin and Boo Mack. We promised to kick it when we got out. Art Lepp was gigantic and cut up and he was my boy, as well. Everybody was scared of Art, but one day he and I had a disagreement and we fought in front of the whole pod. It was a good fight. I shocked myself. Devin couldn't believe it. I think Devin was a little scared of Art. I actually thought Devin was soft, until one day one of the older guys stole Devin's Jordans. It takes heart to fight, no matter who you are. Devin came and sat on my bed and asked me, "You got my back?" I responded, "Hell yeah!" We walked a few isles over and Devin demanded his shoes and .he and the older inmate fought. Devin and I were the exact same age. He stood up for himself and even though he had a black eye, he got his shoes back as well as his respect from the older guys. Even though I was cool with the older guys I was rolling with Devin.

19

In January and February of 1996, I'd gotten into so much trouble and robbed so many boxes with Tyler and Quinn, they raised my status and rode me out to medium security. "What does a nineteen year old do in the real penitentiary?" is all I kept thinking, while riding to Marion correctional.

When I arrived at Marion, I knew this was the real deal. Everybody had that traditional movie blue jail suit on with the coat with the collar flipped up. It was gigantic and loud. Niggas everywhere. Also, Muslims and big white guys with thunderbolt symbols tattooed all over their bodies. Muslims like on TV with their whole bodies covered, and of course homosexuals everywhere looking like real women and being treated like queens.

The first person I saw was Suave from the hood. He was cleaned up, looking like the Suave I knew from 1987. He knew I would be arriving and he had told all the homies from our section. Ed Boom was there. He was a legend in our section for beating niggas down and chocking them out. Whatever he had to do to win, he won. He respected me instantly due to him looking up to my uncle. Most of the older inmates from our section knew my Uncle Tug and showed me love for that fact.

I was moved to One Dorm, which was supposed to be one of the wildest blocks, but I'd known the drill since juvenile days. Once you settled in, they were all the same. One Dorm was a mixture of old and young. The hardest young guy on the block was Cee Black. He was about twenty-one, a real muscular, dark skin kid from Lakeview. I had never seen him fight but it was rumored that he whooped ass royally. His boys were Tricky and Glyde. They were all from St. Clair. Tricky was my age, but known to have had over 100k, and of course I thought that was a lie. He was a little taller than me and looked exactly like an American Indian.

Glyde was short and fat, a little butterball looking kid. He was a few years older than me, but seemed older than he was. He was always clearly scheming and plotting. The worst type of guy always noticeably playing with your intellect. The majority of the time I hung with my cousin Pee-Dub. He was literally 5' 4", real cut up from gymnastics and looked just like a Spanish immigrant. Pee-Dub repeatedly went to the hole for masturbating while looking at COs. It was nasty to me but it was popular amongst the young cats. They all thought the COs liked it, until they ended up in the hole for sexual conduct.

Marion was a big inside penitentiary. Fights all day and every day. People getting stabbed in the gym and on the yard. Dice games and poker games everywhere and you could smell weed and water on the yard at all time. Guys walked the halls holding hands with Homos. This was jail no doubt! And cigarettes ruled! If you had squares you had money. Considering a pack of cigarettes was $1.85, a box was equivalent to $18. You could get anything with a pack of squares; a joint, chips, pop, Little Debbie's or even get a phone call or two. Shit, you could get your bed moved. The clerks were inmates and they did all the bed moves and pod changes everywhere. Without squares you were nothing, probably equivalent to a man on the streets without money, would be measured.

I was learning swiftly in Marion and not just about jail, but also about people. I saw the best of the best and the richest guys get betrayed by their families, closest friends, wives and girlfriends. I called home months back to find out that Cee-Cee was messing around with Bart from Rawlings. Even though Neeka was my girl when I got locked up, Cee-Cee knew that Bart and I were still okay and that we went way back.

What irritated me the most was the fact that Bart sometimes would be outside South High when I went to pick Cee-Cee up from school, and he would often times tell me how fine she was and how lucky I was. I never thought Cee-Cee would mess with a guy I knew, but Bart was the man and had that bank roll. I learned that status meant everything to most females. No chick wanted a broke mediocre dude and I couldn't blame them.

Neeka was a little different from Cee-Cee. If she did anything like that she was so secretive I never found out. When I went to jail, I left Neeka with my Herringbone chain thinking that was her way of representing me. That was stupid because I found out that she pawned it soon after I was locked up, and moved on. But I was doing time and we were young.

The time went so fast in there you forgot about the girls outside, at times. Plus, juvenile prepares you slightly for the disappointments. In Marion, I met some major players. I always heard that jail was the place to expand in the underground world and even though I was still a teen I could recognize money and capitalize off of an opportunity. And again, everyone liked Little Chris.

One dorm was like a circus. There was card games, gambling and drugs constantly being sold. I had a year in and two to go. Shooting dice was my thing. I had learned to pad roll at an early age and we shot dice on blankets when the lights went out. Everybody's money was always on me. I could pass ten consecutive natural seven or elevens. I could make the dice do as I pleased.

One day I was pad rolling against an older guy, Roy Starks, who worked in main laundry. He was about thirty-five, dark skin and about 6' 2" tall with a thick mustache. Roy walked with his chest stuck out at all times and he always carried a knife. He wore his skull cap cocked and his jail suit creased to perfection. If you looked up penitentiary in the dictionary Roy's image should pop up as a lifer, who had already been locked up most of his life.

Roy and I were semi-okay, but one particular day I had beaten him for six boxes of cigarettes. He kept saying, "Keep shooting youngster, I got you," but after two boxes I wanted my cigarettes. I told him to pay me for my two boxes before I continued. Everything got quiet and he told me to go ahead and quit with what I had already won, basically telling me to be happy with what I had won and chalk the new debt.

My respect was everything to me, so I was more furious than anything. Everyone had heard him say this, so I got up and began to commit the ultimate penitentiary violation. I walked to Roy's bed, opened his box where he kept his things and began to look through it for things equivalent to my money. Before I could do anything I felt the hardest flurry of punches come from behind. Before I could retaliate in any manner, of any sort I was being thrown around and punched with great force. All I remember hearing was Dee Black's voice screaming out, "That's a kid. That's a kid Roy, he don't know no better." I felt nothing as I laid on the floor very close to being knocked out.

Several inmates held Roy back as I got up. The whole dorm was quiet and everyone seemed to be shocked and upset. From the other side of the dorm, Roy was being detained as he screamed out, "That's a man. He's grown doing grown man shit and I ain't sparing no nigga that's in here, no matter size or age. If you violate, I'm fuckin you up." I was no match for Roy. He was a man, a real convict. I was a boy who had stepped into another world. The last words from him to me were, "I'll send you home to your mama in a box." All I could do was stare off into the crowd and look at the crew that I was running with as they stood there looking more scared than me. I knew then that those guys weren't anything like me and I knew that in the future I would never ever show another man mercy. I would crush my opponent completely.

John Mann poured the gas on me in Cuyahoga Hills. Roy Starks lit the match. Once Ed and Suave and many others had received the word on what Roy had did everybody under age twenty-seven in the penitentiary from UTW and DTW met in the chow hall to confront Roy and the older guys he ran with. There had to be at least forty guys, some of which I didn't even know, ready to ride for the cause as well as the guys who liked me already. Ed made Roy aware that he couldn't walk the compound anymore without paying me and if anymore fighting would be done it would be done by him. What Ed said was law. Roy paid me the next day without a problem and apologized. I thought it was weird the way everyone respected Ed. Looking at him, you wouldn't think he was tough at all. He was the epitome of what was considered a pretty boy.

For the next few weeks I didn't gamble at all. I watched TV and distanced myself from my dudes. They all had every excuse why they sat back and watched a guy twice my size whoop my ass for literally two minutes. Even when I was soft, I still always helped my dudes. I thought it made me look bad if I didn't help or that if I didn't show true comradeship, I wasn't a friend.

I was walking from the phone and Neeka's mom had just told me Neeka hadn't come home the night before. While walking back to my bed pissed off, I made a mistake and kicked a guy name Down's bed. Down was a loud silly kid who was always joking with his cousin Irv. Before I could apologize he jumped up and loudly screamed out, "I'll beat yo ass worse than Roy." The whole dorm was looking on as he talked and roared. I had no problem with him. He was much bigger than me as well as a few years older. What would or could be gained by starting a fight with me or even beating me up? I was just the little boy who just got beat up by Roy. But in my mind, these guys didn't truly know me. I was Little Lil Chris from 93rd, the fighter, the hustler, the robber, and at that moment I had a point to prove.

As fast as Down began to speak I was on my way back to his bed. I didn't say one word. He had did enough talking for the both of us. I punched him directly in his face and to my surprise he dropped to his knees and I began to weld on him while he tried to get up. When everyone finally broke things up he yelled, "Irv why you ain't help me?" Irv just stood there looking stupid. Irv was my size without near the heart I had. He knew better.

I requested to move right across the hall into Two Dorm, which was much different. I didn't know anybody on Two Dorm except Ed and I remembered Q from Garden Valley. Q was tall, light skin, and super cut-up. He had a mouth like Muhammad Ali and the skills were equal. He was from the same project building as Neeka. When we would play football against the Valley, he was one of the older guys who would be outside cheering for the guys to beat us. Q hung with Jay. They were as different as night and day. Jay was dark skin, about 5' 10" and fat. He was also quiet and laid back. He took care of everybody from the projects. He made sure everyone ate every single day, they ate Big Breaks and Nacho Grandes. At first, I kept to myself when I moved to Two Dorm. Then, one day I seen a guy that I had been locked up with in the county name Ron C. He was from Wade Park. He was tall, dark skin, and ugly with really long, curly hair. He and I would gamble from sun up until sun down. All of his guys from Wade Park were on our dorm, so he was comfortable enough to one day refuse to pay me the money that he owed me. He looked me square in my face and said, "I'm not paying you lil nigga." I didn't say a word. I got up and went to put my shoes on. I'm guessing Q heard what went on, because while I was putting my shoes on, he came over to my bed and asked, "You gone be okay lil nigga?" I barely knew Q, but he knew I was out numbered. He let me know that some of his crew didn't like the Wade Park crew anyway.   He also explained that they weren't going to help if I was going to talk and that was all I needed to hear. I got up and walked over to Ron C and asked him one time, "You got that money?" The look he gave was like, "Didn't I tell you I wasn't paying you?" I started throwing punches without saying anything or giving a warning. Ron C curled up on his bed as I man handled him. He was bigger than me but much weaker. He couldn't even get up. I pounded and pounded until they broke it up. The whole dorm was laughing, mainly because Ron C talked everyday about being this amazing fighter.

That night the embarrassment must have gotten the best of him. His boy Tranelly approached my crew while we were eating and told us that Ron C wanted to fight a fair one. We all went into the bathroom, me and Ron C squared off. I beat him all over the bathroom. A textbook Christian win. He was no match due to him concentrating on slamming me instead of boxing. We all went back to eating like nothing happen. For days, everybody talked about how I whooped Ron C, until Tranelly delivered the same message a few days later. Q, Ed, Ray Ray, and Shorty Brad told me not to do it and that I had nothing else to prove. But I didn't listen. We fought again and I can admit I was flawless until he finally grabbed me and lifted me up high in the sky, then slammed me. I never stopped punching even on the way down but before I could hit the bathroom floor, my back hit the corner of the toilet and I fell between two toilets. Before he could do anymore damage everyone began fighting.

There was a small riot, mostly pushing and shoving. In the mist of all the commotion, Q came to me and whispered in my ear, "Are you okay? You must walk out of here. You can't let them see you get carried". Nobody had noticed I couldn't get up. I couldn't feel my legs. I walked out the bathroom the best I could, but the pain was unbearable. Q eventually told the CO I couldn't walk and they wheeled me out in a wheelchair. I spent a month in the infirmary. I had suffered a very painful herniated disc. I was later released into population still on crutches. I promised myself when I saw him that I would smack him with my crutch. I saw his crew on the yard minus him, but they had a new addition to their crew. It was Pete. He was aware of what had happened and he begged me to leave it alone. I didn't leave it alone because of Pete. I didn't like the hole or the infirmary.

While I was on crutches I was approached by a guy name Lee Terg. I had seen him around the joint working out but mostly minding his business. The word was that he and Sweets were the two best boxing coaches in the place. Terg was my height and somewhere between forty-eight and fifty years old, with long braids and salt and pepper hair. He was athletic built and dark skin. He always talked about training a champion.

The day he approached me he told me he had heard that I'm always fighting and I needed to calm down. I'm thinking, "Old ass nigga. I'm nineteen doing my time." He said, "If you want, I'll train you." I said, "I know the basics pretty well and I've been in the ring a few times. I don't need to know nothing." He laughed and said, "I can show you way better stuff." You could tell he was bored and boxing was his passion, so I agreed. I told him I knew every punch. But he still insisted I start with only footwork. I told him I knew footwork and he told me that I didn't know enough. So we would sprint and do footwork around the track daily. It's ironic, but I never beat Terg in a serious sprint race, and I mean never.

We did so much cardio and footwork I had forgotten what the mission was from start. Terg taught me things I had only seen on TV. He and I got really close. I never got into any fights while I trained. However, I got taller and gained weight. I was probably 150 lbs and about 5' 8". I looked like a totally different person by the time 1997 had approached.

I would see Roy Starks from time to time and the more I saw him the more I respected what he did. It went from total hatred to a smirk on my face whenever I saw him. We never spoke, but I had nothing against him anymore. I got into a few scuffles and beat the guys up and the case manager told Terg he couldn't train me anymore or they would make the parole board aware of his disobedience. He still was willing to train me despite their threats, but I wasn't willing to let him lose parole for me. I had claimed the crown of the hardest red dot (under twenty-one) in the entire Marion Correctional and if you thought different I would accept your challenge. Nobody ever denied the status that I gave myself.

I would always hear about a guy my age named Roro, who had been transferred from Marion before I got there. Everybody respected and feared him. I always wished he would come back so we could fight and then one day when I was coming down the hallway from the gym, I saw a crowd of guys gathered around the new arrivals. I don't know why, maybe from constantly hearing his name, but I felt it in my gut that Roro was back. I walked up to him and asked his name. He looked puzzled before he said, "Roro." He was a handsome kid, about my size but darker and we both had long braids. When he said his name I just walked away. I put it in my head that the first time I heard his name victoriously, I would bust his head.

Weeks went by. Roro was doing his regular I assume. He wasn't fighting. He was just cooling out. Until one day the Crips were outside the library bragging that they had finally caught the one blood they were looking for and they were going to fuck him up. As I walked in the library the only person that was in there was Roro, all by himself, but he didn't look scared. I asked him if he was a Blood and he said that he was. He knew the situation and he seemed ready but unsure. I hated bullies, so I told him, "I'm not in a gang, but I'm a Blood today" sarcastically.

When the Crips came in I told them I was a Blood too. They all began to moan and squeal about how they knew that I wasn't a Blood, etc., and how they didn't want problems with my boys. I went back to Seven Dorm where I had been transferred and all of my crew put on red rags and went out to fight the Crips. It ended up being my dude Mann Buttons from Parkwood representing the Bloods and fighting their leader the Crips' leader, which was Deuce at the time. Mann looked no different than in Indian River. He beat Deuce all over the yard and not a Crip moved to help him. I had friends in both gangs. I just hated guys who took advantage of others. Roro and I were cool from then on. He was from Canton, but he was smooth. He seemed more like a Clevelander. The crown for being the toughest red dot didn't mean so much that day. It felt better being able to help the underdog at that moment.

20

A lot of names I had only heard in the streets, so I had never actually been able to put a face with them, but the stories I heard always had me intrigued about certain guys. I met JB, Skip, Lil Kurt, Q and Jay and countless others. Those were the most notables because I heard the most stories about them.

JB was from Harvard and he was equivalent to Golden down our way. I had heard his name constantly in the streets since 1991. He was young and everyone knew JB. He was tall, brown skin and sort of a big dude, but soft spoken. I could tell that the only reason the guys his age had a little respect for him was because he had money. But JB was real polished. He always talked about his dad, who worked at Ford and helped him get all the newer Fords before they even hit the streets. JB and Golden were the first guys with the new Land Cruisers. Shit they were the only guys with them. I always wanted to meet JB because we had a mutual friend named Brenda. She was five years older than I was and she was JB's girl. Brenda watched me grow up. She would always call me her little boyfriend. She had three fine ass sisters and their momma was even fine. They all looked different, but due to Brenda being half Puerto Rican she was the finest of the sisters. While working at Cermaks, I'd met the whole family. They stayed directly across the street from the pharmacy and at least one of them came in the store every day. When I was finally old enough to hold a decent conversation with Brenda she would always talk about her boyfriend JB. I would look over from Cermaks and see JB pulling up in different cars, regularly and he also was messing with the finest girl from our section, which was Diane.

Diane was one of my best friend's sister. She was brown skin with hazel eyes. Between her and Brenda, I don't know who was the finest. I had lusted for them both since the age of ten. I knew whoever JB was he was the man for real. Skip was the exact opposite of JB. They were the same height, complexion and almost the same build. Skip may have been about three years older than JB, but he had a ruthless reputation. All I had ever heard about Skip was that he killed and robbed people. Skip's total appearance didn't fit his reputation. He even talked softly. But when he came around, it seemed like everyone got quiet while his presence spoke volumes. And if his name came up while he wasn't around nobody would dare speak negative about him.

Skip use to always ask me why I kicked it with JB. He said JB was a bitch and not the type of nigga I should look up to. Skip was rumored to have millions of dollars. He was nonchalant about everything. He was married. When I asked him did he think his wife was gettin' fucked he replied, "I don't care, I'm doing time and she has a pussy. As long as she handles my business." I thought he was crazy for that but it actually made sense. Skip was my type of dude, but JB was as well. JB would always say, "It's not how large you live, but how long you live large." I learned a lot from them both.

Lil Kurt was from my section. He was older than JB but younger than Skip and Kurt didn't like neither of them for real. Kurt was shorter than me with real broad shoulders and a size thirteen shoe. He was light skin with hazel eyes and he was a nice lookin' clean cut guy. Lil Kurt was an outlaw. Nobody liked him at all. He spoke his mind. Kurt was one of those guys who lived by the street code to the death. He wasn't the best fighter, but he wouldn't back down. With a gun he was a monster. He ran with a crew of killers who were commanded by an older cat name Bobo, a legend from my section who had consecutive life sentences, supposedly for drugs, several robberies, and murders. Kurt was one of his henchmen.

JB fit the description of the stories I had heard of him, but Kurt and Skip did not. Nonetheless, I liked them all equally for different reasons.

21

I was transferred back and forth from Two Dorm to Seven Dorm. Those dorms were in the same unit and they were the most fun. I knew a lot of dudes on each dorm, but I stayed fighting and gambling. I never lost another fight or even came close. I slapped guys and spit on 'em. Physically I had become the guy I always wanted to be, not just a dog but a top dog. Respected amongst the top dogs. I was soon to be released and the only thing I was focused on was getting money. I had done so much dirt in Marion, I was locked up and put in the hole for a few weeks.

One early morning, an older Muslim guy came back to the hole and said that he saw the transfer slip and I was on it. I didn't believe him, but when I asked him where I was going he said "LUCASVILLE." The whole range was quiet. I laughed and said, "You lying. I'm only medium security. They can't skip a whole security level to maximum." He replied by saying, "Like I always tell y'all, these honkeys do what they want."

At 5:30 am, the captain came and ironically I saw Q and a lot of other inmates outside the gates who weren't supposed to be there to wish me well on my new journey. The captain gave me a speech about staying hard no matter what and not letting the stories about Lucasville scare me. All the guys told me how much they respected me and we promised to stay in touch. I only had six months left. I was twenty years old. I was nervous, but I pretty much had this jail stuff figured out. Respect meant everything. Win, lose or draw. When it was time to go, it was time. No matter the size or how many. Disrespect had no size or color. It would have to be dealt with at that time. My respect could never be compromised. Ever!

The ride to SOCF was long. It was all the way south near West Virginia. I remember being shackled, thinking, "Damn, I didn't receive a visit my whole three years." I knew I wouldn't get one now. The time had went so fast I just wanted to finally get it over with. I remember when my granny was in her forties, now she was in her sixties. My Aunt Gale had moved right before I left into a nice big house and I had just heard before I was transferred that she had purchased the new Expedition, as well. Besides that, nothing had changed with the family. Tug was locked up right across the street from Marion in North Central. We wrote each other frequently. It was always good to hear from him. He was sending mom more money home than she needed. I lived off gambling, a money order from time to time, and whatever else I could. Both of my boys Tito and Sammy were ballin' really hard. Tupac was dead and Mike Tyson was biting off ears. I couldn't wait to get home.

This was my third time being incarcerated since age fifteen and I was approaching twenty-one. Raymone was incarcerated and we wrote regularly. I found out from the first mail call when I arrived to Lucasville, that Boo Baby had been released. He wrote and sent photos. When I got to Lucasville it was cleaner than I expected. Guys from Toledo, Dayton and Cincinnati that I knew from juvenile, were calling my name, "Hayward. Hayward, Mighty Mouse," etc. Everyone just repeated the cycle I guess. From juvenile to maximum security.

I met guys like Suggie, who had escaped death row. I met reckless cats like 55 who would never see daylight again and just wild out, constantly throwing shit and piss, and stabbing folks for nothing. I met Big O, the biggest guy in Lucasville, and I hadn't seen Ray C since I was fifteen and he sent me a care package.

One of my closest friends Darnell Jackson, D-Rock was there. He had a life sentence. It seemed like I had just saw him on the streets. Darnell was vicious and it caught up to him. He had several murders as a teen, and escaped from DH. When they caught him he received ten extra years for that.

I got into one fight in Lucasville and the guy spit in my face, I beat him up before the spit even touched my nose. I got into it with 55 and he threatened to stab me. Every older guy in the unit told him he couldn't walk the compound if he touched me due to the fact, I was about to go home in 90 days and I didn't know any better.

I turned twenty-one years old right before I went home. I met a Mexican, but I forgot his name. Everybody would tease him because he was in his bad stages of HIV. They would call him a fag. One day we had a conversation and he told me that he did have AIDS, but not from a man. We talked every day. He was from Los Angeles, and in 1991, he'd been caught with a lot of kilos of cocaine. He was sure to die in jail. But he was fine with that matter because his two sons had taken over his drug legacy.

I remembered all the important things that people taught me and one thing the Mexican would always tell me was, "Remember Chris, if u are not tripling your money, you ain't hustling and to make money, you gotta hit the road. A true hustler goes where the dope is and says fuck a middle man." At first, I didn't understand him because I always doubled my money in the crack game. I couldn't imagine a triple up. My uncle would always say, "You need to sell heroine if you just have to hustle," and I had noticed that heroine was what all the wealthiest young guys and older rich guys were into.

Suggie would talk to me day in and day out as well. He would always say, "Avoid conflict and eliminate stress. A weak mutha fucka can never disrespect a strong nigga. It's impossible." He would always school me about the importance of not touching nothing and letting other people do all my dirty work, etc. A lot of things I couldn't grasp mentally leaving Lucasville.

Brenda wrote me my entire three years that I was incarcerated. I told JB she was sending me money and nice photos. I thought he was stand up, but he told her everything I discussed with him about her. I learned that sometimes it doesn't matter about the money when it comes to women. JB had all the money in the world but Brenda still treated me like a boss and I didn't have a penny. He looked at me as being beneath him at the time, so he couldn't accept the fact. Brenda told me, "Don't kiss and tell," and I learned that men are just as emotional as women.

I learned early in life that having money doesn't make you a real nigga, and it damn sure doesn't make you strong and respect worthy. I learned to have a certain love for the people who taught me things, putting their flaws to the side. I left Lucasville December 17th, 1997. I was twenty-one years old. In the last six years I had transformed totally. I was ready. I caught the bus home and it was a long ride that seemed to take forever. I remember the bus driver screaming out, "Next stop 18th and Chester." I jumped off the bus while it was still moving it seemed. I saw my grandmother and Gale waiting. I was happy, but this was the first time my grandmother had ever looked old to me. She told me that people had been calling and coming over all day awaiting my arrival. It was already 10 pm and she didn't want me leaving out, but I was going anyway. When we got home, Gale gave me six nice French braids to the back. Boo-Baby and the rest of the neighborhood were outside waiting on me. We were going to the Mirage on the Water.

After all the hugs and daps, I asked Boo-Baby to take me to Cee-Cee's house. When I arrived I was met at the door by her mom and she actually seemed happy to see me, but she had a disgusted look on her face and pointed toward upstairs. So I knew Cee-Cee was upstairs. When I went in Cee-Cee's room she was throwing up and crying. I was in disbelief wondering what was wrong. She was in love with another guy, and she was pregnant. I told her that it could just be me and her if she had an abortion, but she was in love. She said she would think about it. She was only about six weeks, but I could tell she was set on having the baby. When I was leaving, CC's mom begged me to make her have the abortion. I was so happy that I was home that when I walked out that house, I didn't look back. I don't think I saw Cee-Cee again until after she had the baby. Actually, I was hunting for Kimmie and Brenda. Kimmie had a boyfriend but I knew where her heart was. She was thorough, any guys' dream girl. She was of course still a woman, but she was loyal to the highest degree and she always carried herself like a lady with class and polish. Brenda was 26 with a degree, a great job and everything else. Neeka was just fine as ever. I got along with them all. I knew me and Brenda would never be. She was always like a fantasy to me.

I went to the Mirage with my hood and my dude Vern Bridge, who I had met in jail. I nicknamed him Snoop because he looked exactly like the rapper with his braids, as well as his demeanor. Snoop was two years older than me with an older brother, Mill. When I wasn't training with Terg in Marion, I was hanging out with Snoop. One time, when I went to the hole, Snoop beat a guy's ass who owed me while I was back there. He wasn't doing well yet because he had just gotten out about a month before me. But Snoop was a hustler.

That night at the door while entering the Mirage, I saw Golden. He and his crew were still reigning supreme like always. I also saw my boy Bob from the School of Science and he was ballin' major. He was looking like a million bucks and bragging about buying kilos. He would tell everybody, "This the nigga that gave me my first rock and showed me how to hustle," and then point to me. We all partied and had a great time.

Eventually, I went home and as soon as I woke up Tito picked me up from my grandmother's. Everyone knew I was home. He had the new Eddie Bauer Explorer and a lot of other cars. He took me shopping and bought me everything he said he would wear, if he was flashy. Tito was weird and that would never change. He gave me $1000 and told me to call him when I was ready to hustle. Then, the next day Sammy picked me up. I had heard several stories of Sammy's come up, but he looked normal. He was driving a regular Blazer and he had on a Dickie suit and a Carhartt jacket. But when we drove off I noticed something different about him. Before I left his front teeth had been knocked out and now his smile was perfect, but the teeth were gold with huge diamonds on every tooth. Sammy would always amaze people. He was a perfectionist. The ultimate hustler. We rode off laughing as I mentioned the gold teeth. I was happy for him. We rode up Kinsman, turned right on Lee road and went in to Equalizer Electronics and we were looking at all the cars in there. The best car in there was a '96 Impala SS on 20" rims. The rims looked bigger than me. As I kept talking about this car with the TVs, Sammy hit the chirp to let me know it was his, and we laughed even harder. I didn't know what the car was or what size the rims were or how and why he had all the TVs everywhere. It was 1997 and I had been gone almost three years. All this stuff was new. The whole world had changed. From there we went to Beachwood Mall and Sammy bought me everything I wanted and anything he thought was fly. We rode and he told me to make sure I called him so we could bring in the New Year together. He pulled out a bag of dope bigger than any bag I had ever seen. It had to be at least twenty six ounces. He offered me an eighth (4.5 ounces) out of the bag. I told him I wasn't ready just yet, so he gave me $500 dollars and sped off.

Things were looking good. I had only been out three days. I had a wardrobe and a small bank. I heard loud music playing outside. It was, "We No Limit Soldiers, I thought I told ya (Bitch get your mind right!!)" was the lyrics that I heard. I looked out and saw what appeared to be a spaceship with gold rims sitting outside. I knew it was for me. It was Bob. I ran out and jumped in the car with him, light skin Don and Baby Ray. We rode downtown to the Millennium Nightclub on the brick street. The club was going berserk. It was clear that Bob was the man. He was a young boss.

After the club, we went to Bob's house He had moved upstairs into what use to be his blind grandfather's home. He had truly updated the house. It was fresh. He even had fish tanks in his walls. Bob was fly to be only twenty-one, and he wore Gators and Mink coats. The next morning he took me on a shopping spree. He wasn't as generous as Sammy and Tito, but he looked out. When he dropped me back off at home, I kept thinking, "I've been out of jail for four days already and I still hadn't gotten any pussy," which was funny because right at that moment Brenda called while I was doing push-ups. She asked me if I could come outside, sarcastically in reminiscing of when I was sixteen and she would joke about me not being old enough to stay out all night. Fifteen minutes later she was at my door and I was happy as hell to see her.

Brenda and I arrived at an amazing three thousand square foot home that I later found out she shared with some rich guy. We watched TV and laughed and talked about her watching me grow up at the drug store. We reminisced as well about my smart mouth. I don't know how it happened but we ended up naked. I was nervous because she was older, and it was Brenda She wasn't just my fantasy, she was everybody's fantasy. We licked on each other then I went down on her. I had only ate two girls out in my life before her. I licked and sucked over and over before she stopped me and began to guide me. She told and showed me how to please her. I still remember her voice saying, "Forget all the sucking hard and fast licking. It's this thing right here and it's just the gentlest touch." We had great sex. I spent the night and she took me home in the morning.

22

Everyday was an adventure. I had clothing and money. I was doing well. I started back dating Neeka about a week or two after I got out. She had a decent job and she bought me a 1986 Box Chevy. It was tan and maroon, two-toned and super clean. I hadn't been out of jail two weeks yet. Abercrombie and Fitch was getting hot. She bought me a bright yellow ski coat. I guess she felt guilty for falling off and selling my chain, but that shit was old. I had known Neeka my whole life. The first time we went out she said, "I suck dick now and I'm good at it." I use to beg Neeka for some head before I went to jail, but she wouldn't put a dick near her mouth. We were grown now and she was finer than ever. We would roll together all day, every day. But some nights she would disappear and I wouldn't hear from her. I thought it was fishy, but it didn't matter. She had looked out and girls were calling my granny's house 24/7.

New Year's Eve came around and Sammy let me use his new Blazer, so I cruised around all day feeling like I had some money, listening to all Tupac and No Limit. Right before the clock struck midnight, I stopped at Kimmie's house.

Kimmie was doing really well. She was only twenty years old and she was waiting on her first house to close. She was a part-time, real estate agent now and the manager at a check cashing place. A lot had changed. Sometimes watching Kimmie made me realize that I knew I could do better with my life, but the streets was easy money. Even though Cleveland was the jungle, when you're raised in the wild, it doesn't seem so bad. You start not to even notice all the robbing, shootings, killings, etc., it becomes normal. After me and Kimmie had reminisced for a few hours, I received a page from Sammy, letting me know that it was almost New Years. Time had went so fast while I was talking to Kimmie that I had lost track.

Sammy lived smack dab in the hood in a two-family home. When we went upstairs his house was plushed out like a King's palace. Today, if I didn't believe that he had the money I heard he had, I knew it was true. Sammy took me into a room and there was over $200,000 dollars on the floor. He had three AK 47s and he showed me how to load them. We loaded all three. Sammy had on a Mink coat, a Coogi sweater and Gator boots. He was always clean even when we were children, but now he was on another level. He was pissy drunk when he told me, "Chris, I'm gone put you on but remember somebody always gone want your spot. Trust nobody." He began talking about putting a Corvette motor in his SS Chevelle and bragging about his new Harley. At the time, I was twenty-one and he was twenty-four. He was talking drunk talk to me, but for real, he was way ahead of his time. We went outside and shot all three machine guns until they were so hot we threw them in the yard and watched the guns melt the snow.

Sammy tried to make me take a drink, but I refused. We talked until about 3 am. When we went upstairs to put the guns away, I noticed a change. There was a female in the house and a gigantic black pit bull. I said Sammy put the dog up. He said, "A dog will not bite around its master." The female had freckles on her face with a big gap in her teeth, but despite the freckles, she was still super bad. She looked exotic, right out of a fuckin magazine. She was damn near naked, but Sammy was a show off. He didn't care. He wanted me to see that she was bad. Once he introduced us, I knew that was my cue to start heading out.

We said our goodbyes and I drove over to Mt. Auburn to Martin Hearts' house. Martin's family had moved from 93rd. They didn't move too far, Mt. Auburn was located in Section Three. The Hearts' house was like always, the absolute party house. Ms. Heart never cared. It was like our home. Martin's brothers were around sixteen and eighteen now. The Hearts had all three floors.

Larry's grandmother owned a house next door and that's where Larry was living. While I was gone Larry had a son. He was always mature for his age, but now he got on my nerves. He never wanted to play like when we were teens anymore. I seemed to irritate everyone these days. I was real serious in the streets, but around my partners I was a child. I spent that whole day at the Hearts home. Cordell, Chunk and Buddy Bonneville all came over because they hadn't seen me yet. Boo-Baby also came over. There was about thirty of us and we had a ball. That was the day I took my first drink. It was Hennessy. Chunk betted me that I couldn't drink a whole pint without staggering. I believed in the expression "mind over matter" so I betted and I actually won the bet. As soon as I finished drinking it, Buddy and I had plans to leave. Chunk paid up and me and Buddy left.

Buddy was only eighteen, but while I was gone, he had a baby as well. He was proud to take me to his new house and he talked about his girl and son the whole time on the ride there. He was sharp for his age. As soon as we pulled up his first words were, "Chris please don't tell nobody where I live." I gave my word and I never did.

Buddy use to buy double ups from me secretly when he was only eleven or twelve. He was smooth and quiet. I figured he would be great one day. Even though he wasn't ballin', he still managed to take me shopping anyway. He was the type of guy who pockets you could never count, but he clearly had more than all the guys my age. Shit all of us were mostly still living at home. Buddy had a nice Monte Carlo SS with T-tops, and a Toronado. When we pulled up to his house, I opened the door to get out and as soon as I stood up, I fell flat down on my face, like a pancake. I couldn't get up and walk for nothing in the world. I kept laughing. I was paralyzed. But the funny thing was that I liked the feeling. Buddy laughed hard as ever and carried me into his house. I slept the liquor off. Then, in the middle of the night he woke his son up to show him to me. They were identical. You could tell that was his joy. Even though I didn't have or want kids at the time. It was a beautiful sight. Buddy was a little man in my eyes. We all knew Buddy wasn't a fighter or had never been a shooter or any of that. He was just Buddy and the block loved him as he was.

I began to meet up with Buddy more often. He had just got out of high school, so he had the straight shot to all the seventeen to twenty year old females. My dude Lil Ant, was in his senior year in high school. He was a little pretty boy who had walked the neighborhood playing basketball since the age of five, literally. Everyone in the neighborhood knew Ant. His grandmother was Muslim. She was like a mother to all of us. Ant had several uncles, the Kendricks' and they all looked exactly alike. They all had hazel eyes.

His uncles were real close to my uncles. I'd only have to describe one of Ant's uncles, to have described them all. They were all light skin around 6' tall. There was P.J., Yellow, Rev and everyone's favorite Bo.

Bo was half crippled, but he was down. He sold dope and cooked it for you. Everyone shot dice at Bo's house ever since I could remember. He would always tell me that I was his favorite, out of a whole block of 100 boys. We had a great relationship. We borrowed money from each other and although, Bo was never rich, he kept a hustle going all day, every day. There was always something going on over on Anderson, at his house. When necessary, we ran from the police to his house. He was an outlaw. Everyone got good advice from Bo and he never took sides. When I started hustling he told me, "Chris, you will be the greatest they've ever seen." I never understood that, but Suave and Ben Hynsley always told me the same thing. I just thought that they were trying to get some free drugs. But Bo didn't use drugs, so he had no motive. That was his opinion, I guess. But with Bryan and a few others doing so well, I didn't even see that myself.

That year, Snake had the block on lock. He also lived on Anderson, across the street from Lloyd and Isaac. Lloyd was wild as hell. Both he and Snake were a year younger than me. When I went to jail Snake was shorter than me, but when I got out he was 6' 3". He had a sister name Marie and a brother, Golan who was mentally ill. Snake was real silly, tall, dark brown skin and didn't have any front teeth. He would crack jokes on everybody even though he was snagga tooth. This was the new crew, my old crew had fell off. Little Sal, Ali, Buddy, Jack, Lloyd, Cordell and myself hung out.

We stayed on the block all day. Little Sal was about fifteen when I went to jail. He was the youngest of us all, but he was tough. This crew was dynamite. Except for Buddy and Ant, we were all great fighters. Buddy and Ant would fight just because they knew they had to help.

23

It was February 1998. After being out about two months and hustling in the cold weather with my boys, Sammy and Tito had put me in position. I had begun to drink daily. I didn't think anything was wrong with it, even though my mom was an alcoholic. I didn't consider myself out of my character because I was actually still working out. I said, "I could never be an alcoholic I'm twenty-one, having fun." One day, I went home and my grandmother had found a large bag of rocks in my room. She didn't curse me out. She just said she wanted me out of her house. I packed my things with nowhere to go, but I had a car and I was hustling swell. I began to drive up the street and I got a thought, "Raymone was still in jail." His mom loved me so I stopped and knocked on the door and told her that my granny had put me out. She welcomed me with open arms. She said I could stay for two months until I got myself a place. I was happy so I agreed to her terms.

Raymone's two little sisters were now fourteen and seventeen. The seventeen year old, Ria, was friends with Buddy's girlfriend. So, sometimes we would all go out together. Raymone's mom never suspected anything. She went to work daily at 5 am. I slept in the living room. It was comfortable there. Just like when we were children. There was always food and she kept all the latest gadgets. Everyone in the house was dark skin and they all had pearly white teeth, including Ria. She and I were more friends than anything and she had a lot of friends that frequented the house. When Raymone's mom went to work they would all come over. Ria was thick with real long curly hair. She had a nice body, big tits and a flat stomach. Raymone asked me to never mess with her and I gave him my word that I wouldn't. Even though Raymone and I had bad arguments and fall outs from time to time, I still considered both him and Larry my brothers.

One morning, I was laying on the floor and Ms. Rivers had just left for work. Ria came in the living room with a short shirt on. I thought I was seeing things but I could clearly see her ass and cooch. She said, "You can sleep in the bed with me if you like." I was shocked and in disbelief. But at twenty-one, of course my hard dick beat me out. I jumped up and sprinted to the room behind her. I was excited. Her body was so warm and thick. I just remember between her legs being soak and wet. We tried to have sex that day and every day after. She was so tight it was unbelievable. For a week she even lied and claimed to be a virgin but I knew different because her old boyfriend had went to South High with my whole crew. In fact, our whole neighborhood had been transferred to South, due to John Adams closing down. Ria and I finally managed to make the sex thing work. We would have sex five times a day. And I was still going with Neeka. I told Neeka that I still lived with my grandmother and everything worked out fine. Kimmie had a steady boyfriend, so we only snuck and talked once or twice a week. Ms. Rivers still didn't have a clue. Around the house, Ria and I acted as if we weren't even on speaking terms. Just hi and bye.

My life was amazing. And I don't know if it was because I did time, because I had been to Lucasville or because everyone had heard about me the last five or six years. But I had major stripes. I noticed guys were scared of me and the guys that I ran with. Snake could knock you silly with one punch. Cordell would beat you to death. Ali would shoot u dead in broad daylight. Lloyd was a maniac and Sal, he was just a baby. No facial hair or nothing but he would destroy multiple guys at a time. I would just beat you for ten minutes without you getting the chance to hit me back. I would make you quit. I fought to embarrass. I was young and fast. But most importantly, I was fearless. I accepted every challenge and if I felt disrespected one bit, I'd knock you out clean before you seen it coming. We all stayed at go and we never backed down.

Ali, Bryan, and I still liked to rob folks. We snatched chains and anything else. Our block was treacherous. On nights that I didn't have dope, I would team up with junkies like Big Les or Gary Goon and we would rob every dope boy outside in the am. Big Les would strip them while I held the gun and Gary Goon would do the same. I was actually more comfortable hitting licks with Big Les than my dudes. Les and Gary was two of Tug's best friends growing up. Even though we were committing robberies, I could feel the loyalty they had for my uncle and the will to make sure I was safe.

Every day a different crew rode down Anderson looking for one of us, for something we had done. Our whole block smoked the drug PCP, except me and a few others. But we would lie and say I did as an excuse for all of my scandalous actions. I sold crack and did small robberies. I thought I was invincible.

One day, I was riding with Pretty Ant and Neeka's little brother Laneer. We were on our way to Teen America, a local boxing club for boys and we were being followed by the police. I had just purchased fourteen grams of crack and being so scared of returning to prison, I began to eat it. The police followed us all the way down West 25th toward where the gym was located. After I had eaten all the crack the police turned off. We laughed about the situation and proceeded into the gym.

We watched on as the trainer, Sajo, worked with all of the best teenage boxers in the city. Laneer was a dog and Sajo had trained him. I had only heard stories of Sajo being the best trainer in the city. After watching for about thirty minutes, I yelled out, "I can beat anybody in this gym," and I believed I could have, since it hadn't been long since I had left the joint. I was still in very good shape. I talked and talked and talked until finally I told Sajo that I could whoop him. The whole entire gym fell silent. At first he was hesitant, so I thought he was unsure of himself, but right before I thought I had captured a small victory he said in a low tone, "Put the head gear on." Then, he looked over to one of his protégés and said, "Set the clock for three rounds." I was pumped. I was ready.

I looked at Sajo. He wore a mail delivery suit because he was also a mailman. He was around my height, dark skin, slim and built like a boxer. He had a square head. He didn't look his age, but I knew approximately how old he was because he had two sons older than me that were boxing when I was younger and just learning to box. The bell rang and we began to go around the ring and fill each other out. We both threw punches. Sajo slipped every punch I threw. The faster I moved, he adjusted and moved just as fast. I had him on the ropes one time and I had thrown six or seven punches and not one of them touched him. The bell rang.

We went to our corners and waited then headed back in for round two. But this time things were different. Sajo came out and punched me directly in the nose very hard and accurate. I remember thinking, "Damn, that hurt."

We began to mix it up a bit, but every time I hit Sajo once, it seemed as though he hit me ten times. He kept cutting the ring off. It began to be a disaster as he chased me around the ring. I was so happy when the bell rang. Everyone in the gym, especially his students, were hollering and laughing. Their coach had destroyed me and we still had another round left to fight. I was crushed and embarrassed but I got back in and fought. It was all one sided. Sajo didn't seem to have broken a sweat. I took the head gear off and left and my boys clowned me for the rest of the day.

About 7 or 8 pm that evening, I had begun to see things that weren't there. I was hallucinating and moving really fast and it felt as if my chest was about to burst wide open. The guys rushed me to the hospital because they knew I had swallowed the crack. I saw the police when we got there and I panicked and left. Once I got back to the hood everything got worse and we all rushed back to St. Luke's Hospital. Most people hated St. Lukes, we thought it was for poor people, but it was right by the hood so that's all we had if you didn't have medical insurance.

Ria rushed straight to the desk in the emergency room and told the receptionist that I had swallowed crack and that I needed immediate attention. A black doctor assured me that the police wouldn't be involved. At that time, I would have rather died than go back to jail. The doctors strapped me down and made me aware that my stomach would have to be pumped and they went ahead with the procedure. It was painful. Every time they pumped it felt like they were taking my soul. The doctor showed me all the cocaine at the top of the bag after the extra substance had been eaten off of the chemicals. Then, he told me I could have died. I didn't grow up in the church, but that was one of the first real experiences that made me believe firmly in a higher power. I heard of guys dying from eating only a few rocks. I had eaten fourteen grams of crack without plastic and then went and got my head beaten in afterwards, and I was still here.

     The next day while recovering I received an unexpected visitor. My boxing coach from jail "Terg". He preached about me being a natural and how he could make me a champ, etc. I didn't want to hear it. I hadn't seen Terg in over a year and in my opinion, I was doing great. I was twenty-one, I had my respect and I was moving a package and taking shit regularly. This was the best I had ever lived and all I had ever known. The block was my family and in my mind, we were on top. I told Terg, I would box but I never called him. Terg showed me photos of him in Vegas. All I knew about Vegas is that one of my favorite cousins Mason had been killed there, execution style the year before. Besides Jock from Prince being killed a few years back, those were the first people I knew closely that were murdered.

     I continued beating guys out, robbing, snatching chains and living on the block selling crack. At times, I would migrate to Kinsman to hang with Sammy or call him for work. Sammy was living large. He was only twenty-four years old riding Harley's and driving new everything. He had the

Navigator, Chevelles, Cadillacs on Switches, Four-wheelers, etc. He was on top for real. He would ride around with literally two kilos cut up in every form, from quarter ounces to eighth of keys. He kept two or three scales on him at all times. He was a perfectionist and a genius in the streets.

My dude Tito was the exact opposite. He never rode with a piece of dope. He had nice things but you rarely saw them. Tito never wore anything other than t-shirts and track shoes. No jewels or flashy anything, but he had whatever Sammy had and more. People loved Sammy. People feared Tito.

Tito wasn't friends with anyone. He treated the game serious and like a business. He had houses in all the surrounding suburbs. To me, Sammy and Tito were both fly in their own way. The one thing they both had in common was that they agreed I was a fuck up. They didn't agree with the robberies and me fuckin my money off and even though I justified my actions, I knew I should be further along than I was. Not because I had been hustling as long as they had, but because I had better connections than both of them, or just as well. I had booked everybody that could serve me and would front me. Bob from Superior and Devin from Tarkington were both ballin'. Vernell Queen, Tricky from St. Clair, and Ike from Gaylord was ballin'. Everybody I started this game with was getting real money, except me. Golden was still the reigning champ. That year he had the 500 S Class Benz. He never missed a beat. There were guys getting' money that I knew should not have had a dime.

It was 1998 when 20" wheels came into play and only a few guys had them. Sammy was the first one I had ever seen with them and Warren from the projects down on 30th had them on a brand new Eldorado, and a guy name Fred from Tarkington had them on a white Lexus.

Sammy was very silly. Sammy would always tease me when I went to him asking to be put back on my feet, but he never denied me. It could be a free ounce or a fronted eighth. He always wanted to see me on top. Even if I owed him he would still bless me. Tito would do the same, but he was violent and we would have arguments when I fucked the money up. I know Tito didn't fear me but he knew I wouldn't go out easy without a fight and he was known for humiliating guys.

That summer, I found out that Neeka and Ria were both pregnant the same week. I didn't know how to feel. I was shocked, scared and unsure. But the biggest thing was that I was unstable and only juggling about $4000 to $5000. I wasn't a real baller. I was actually doing worse than I was doing as a teen, but my fronts were up better. I had jewelry, cars, and I kept up with all the latest fashion, etc., but I kept my whole stash on me. Hearing the news about the pregnancies had changed my whole way of thinking. I was still drinking a little and I had no clue or direction. All I knew was that I was free and in the streets.

I went over Neeka's house one day to find out that she had had an abortion. She was in the bed crying and telling me she wasn't ready. I understood and to be honest, I was kind of relieved. Ria on the other hand didn't believe in abortions. She was in her last year of high school. I had to be ready. My thoughts were, "in seven months from now, I'll have my shit together and I'll be on top."

24

One night I went over to the Hearts' with Larry to hangout and like always there were at least thirty people in the house. Jimbo had a bunch of young females over there that all looked to be between the ages of fifteen and eighteen. We all had our pick. I picked Gee Gee, a brown skin, real pretty girl with curly hair and a pretty smile. She looked like a little Dominican. I started talking to her and one thing led to another. I took her next door to Larry's house, but before I did Larry and I made a $100 bet about who would have sex with her first. We had been making bets about everything ever since we were eight or nine years old. I usually won and I was hoping to win this one, as well.

When Gee Gee and I got to Larry's we talked, but of course I only had one thing on my mind. I tried to get her to give me head but she refused several times. In my mind I would always revert to that day in study hall when I asked Golden, "How do you make a girl give you head," and he said, "Just pull yo dick out and put their head down there." I hadn't had much oral sex at the time. But when I did get it, I loved it. I was blessed down low so it was always exciting to watch girls try to get the whole thing in their mouth. Gee Gee wouldn't even put it near her mouth. So instead we had sex and I was happy with that.

Gee Gee smoked weed and that would always loosen her up. I told Larry that I had won the bet and he paid me. I had sex with Gee Gee for a week straight. She bled the first few times, then it was normal, and even though she was young, she caught on real fast. She hung with a crew of girls including a crew of triplets who were just as wild and fine. Gee Gee's crew were all light skin and nicely shaped. Two of the triplets were identical and the other one was equally fine. The triplets also had an older sister about my age. They lived a few streets down from my block and all of them smoked weed. Gee Gee and one of the twins were very close and were always together. I think they were poor because one day while we were all kickin it at me and Snake's dope house the only thing in the house to eat was Ramen Noodles and Gee Gee and the triplet both ate three or four soups a piece.

Gee Gee and I had sex a few more times at her house. Her mom was cool with me being there. She even made us food while she told us old stories about the '70s and I would laugh at her stories. She looked like she may have been attractive years back. She was a medium brown complexion, tall and slim with wild, curly hair all over her head. However, now she was in bad shape, physically. She looked to be a junkie of some kind, but I wasn't sure of her drug of choice.

I went to Minnesota that summer for a month to visit my family. That was my first time out of the state and I had a ball. My cousins who were less clever in the streets than I was were actually major players up in the twin cities. During my visit they were showing me how the guys up there paid double what we paid for everything and how I could make triple what I made in Cleveland. Broke or not I always kept my antennas up for the money and I knew I would always remember Minnesota, the twin cities. It was tougher than I thought. It wasn't like Cleveland but it was far from soft.

When I returned home from visiting my family, everyone was telling me that a lady was looking for me that looked like a dope fiend. They said she was telling everybody I owed her money. A few days passed and I was on Anderson when a tan Bonneville pulled up. The ones that looked like a Cutlass (the 1984 to 86 ones). Then Trice (Gee Gee's mom) jumped out and said, "Get into the car and let me talk to you." As, I approached the car, I saw that Gee Gee was hunching down in the front seat. She was crying looking embarrassed and terrified. I sat in the back seat. Trice showed me some papers stating that Gee Gee had been caught stealing from CVS. I didn't think that was my problem. Then she explained that Gee Gee was stealing a pregnancy test and I knew where this conversation was going. So I instantly said, "That ain't my baby!" She said, "tell him," and "Gee Gee whispered, "I was a virgin." I didn't believe her. When I met her, she was drinking and smoking, etc., but that wasn't the bad part. Trice hollered, "Tell him how old you are," and Gee Gee said, "thirteen." I didn't even care. I just wanted out the car. I didn't believe any of it. A few days later Trice pulled up again. This time she was alone with an affidavit stating that on Gee Gee's last doctor's appointment she was a virgin and that she was as of this day six weeks pregnant and that she had stolen the pregnancy test because she had missed her period. Trice asked me for money for an abortion and I told her I would pay her the next day.

I thought everything was cool and the situation was handled until the next day when Trice pulled up. I offered her $400 and she refused it. She stated that she wanted $5,000 because I didn't believe her at first. At first I thought she was tripping, but her face was cold hearted as ever. Trice carried herself like a street guy from the 70s.

When I saw that Trice was serious I tried to use the mind trick by saying, "You're going to mess up your daughter's life." She didn't care. Her greed, plus opportunity had kicked in. But I had no intentions on paying more than what the abortion cost. Weeks went by and Trice constantly harassed me. She went to my grandmother, my aunt and even my pregnant girlfriend demanding that they convince me to give her the money or she would report the situation to the police.

She stole things out of my cars while they sat on the streets and she told everybody in the neighborhood I had a bag of fake dope. This went on for about a month until I finally told her, "I'm not giving you anything. Go to the police". Larry and I were riding up Miles one day and we saw Gee Gee walking. Larry told me to pick her up, so I did. Her stomach was visible. I felt bad because she wanted to have the baby but I didn't agree. She was too young to be a mother and I already had a baby on the way. I picked her up and asked her how she was doing. She said she was okay, that she was scheduled to get an abortion from the county, and that her mom was going to have to press charges on me in order to receive payment for an abortion from the county.

When we dropped Gee Gee off, Larry looked me in the face and said, "That's one bet I'm glad I lost." Days went by and she kept me updated on what was going on. Then one night she called and told me that she'd had the abortion. I felt relieved and I told her that I was sorry. She told me that the detectives said they were looking for me. I didn't think it was that serious. I was just happy she wasn't pregnant anymore.

My uncle had just gotten out of jail and he analyzed my entire scene and the company I was keeping, and as usual I received heavy criticism. And also, as usual, I didn't see what he saw. Tito was fronting me nine ounces and Marty was fronting me another nine ounces. I was hittin' my whole squad off. Things were starting to look good.

Winter was approaching. I was twenty-two years old and I had a baby on the way, and I wasn't on papers, so I was winning. But in my uncle's eyes I was hanging with a bunch of losers who smoked wet all day, that wasn't serious about the dope game, and who would tell on me the first chance they had. I believed that my uncle was always too harsh with his thoughts and opinions, but he was my uncle.

Marty would preach the same things to me as my uncle. He was one of our neighborhood's worse junkies when I first started hustling and he said he always liked me because I was one of the only younger hustlers who always treated him with respect. Marty was short, skinny, and dark skin and despite his past addiction, he was actually now the richest guy in the hood besides Quo. And he showed his respect by always giving me extra grams or fronting me whatever I purchased. At this particular time I had two dope houses in the neighborhood. One on 98th and Benham and the other on Benham, on the same side of the street but a few blocks up closer to 103rd.

I had begun implementing all of the things that I'd learned in jail as well as listen to my uncle. The drug game was not a game. My life and freedom was on the line at all times. I had stopped drinking due to the fact that on my birthday I got so drunk I pissed and threw up all over myself and I was embarrassed. I woke up with a headache throwing up and promised God that I would never, ever drink again.

It was the beginning of 1999. Pretty Ant had dropped out of college on a basketball scholarship. Larry and Martin weren't the best hustlers, but they were my loyal friends. I felt I could build with this crew and I did. I operated my drug houses exactly like "Suggie" told me to when I was in Lucasville. No junkies were allowed inside. You either purchased $20 and up by tens; $20, $30, $40, etc. I had runners. Veronica, Big Les, Gary Goon, Mark, Big Ron, and Chill would run all night. I would give them a $20 chop for every $100 they brought me. Ant and Larry would work the corners directing traffic to the houses. Marty would bring me nine ounces every other day or I would go to Sammy or freckle face Barney from Section Two. My whole team was eating. We were wearing Coogi sweaters and Air force Ones, Avirex, and Pelle Pelle leathers. We actually had Semi Trucks pulling up in the middle of the night. I wasn't robbing anymore. The only violence I indulged in was when we were building our clientele. I knocked out every junkie who came with less than $20. Larry and Ant weren't violent. Martin was down for whatever as long as money was involved. Everything was smooth. Things couldn't get better. We had been having this run since October of 1998 and it was February. My son was due in March.

One Saturday morning Martin and I were going to Mary's, the local diner to get breakfast. When we walked in the vice was there eating. We ordered our food and went back outside to wait. When we got back outside, Martin said he noticed the vice looking funny. I was cockier than ever at the time, so I said, "Fuck the police." Martin said that he didn't think it would be a great idea to go back and get the food. I said, "Fuck them, I'm getting my food. I paid for it". Martin and I disagreed a lot growing up. He and quite a few of my other friends always thought more realistic and rational than I did. So, fifteen minutes passed and we went back in to the diner to get our food.

I was always a strong believer in, "Whatever you think into existence will come." I remembered Gee Gee telling me, "The police said they won't look for you you're a drug dealer you'll pop up," but I ignored all that. My logic was that 'it wouldn't be that serious' when I told them that her mom was aware that we were messing around and that Gee Gee had lied about her age. Martin and I grabbed our food and left. I laughed and called him scary.

As soon as we pulled off and approached the intersection of 93rd and Union, everything began to go in slow motion. Unmarked police cars were coming from every angle. All I could do was watch as they surrounded my car. I had just purchased a showroom clean, 4-door Cutlass with raised white letter tires and under the seat was the 9mm, and ninety-six grams of crack that Martin had just begged me not to bring along for the ride. I had license and insurance. Who thought I would be getting pulled over? The police jumped out and opened my door. The traffic light was red and I couldn't run.

I had big plans for that day. It was Black Dre's birthday party and Martin and I had just went shopping the day before. It was one of those sunny winter days when all the snow melts. My life had all crumbled in one second.

The first thing the police asked when they opened Martin's door was, "What's his name?" Martin's reply was, "He has a name ask him." The officer slapped him in the head and slammed him to the ground and cuffed him. At that moment I didn't say another word. The police found the gun and the drugs and then told me I was wanted for sexual assault. Martin and I were taken to the district and he was released the next day. All I could think about was were the dope houses being ran correctly. I was transferred to county and charged.

My lawyer, Stephen Border, told me not to say anything. Stephen was the hottest lawyer in the city. He was a young hotshot lawyer with the bluest eyes and he looked exactly like the chrome cop in the movie, Terminator. He had a reputation for fixing anything. I was issued a $250,000 bond and I told Steph I couldn't pay it. Ten percent was only $25,000 and I couldn't pay that either. Steph told me he could get the bond dropped to $100,000. With the leftover dope, I could pay that. I had been in the county for a week. When they dropped my bond I was $3,000 short, but before I could make a call Sammy had heard the news and straightened the balance. I was released that night.

I went straight to the hospital because my son had been born that morning. I missed my first child's birth. I noticed a lot of the things that my uncle had been telling me just off this one situation. My whole entire hood couldn't come up with the remaining balance of $3000. I had only been gone from the dope houses for eight days and everything had went to pieces. Not only was money short, but at one of the houses some rival dealers had busted out all of the windows.

I learned that to run a business you must be there or at least accessible. I didn't have much money when I got out. After I collected what the crew owed me, I got my car out of impound and sold it for a few thousand. I bought me a Blazer to get around in and got an apartment and a small package.

Once again, I had a case and everything was different. I needed to take life more serious and maturely. My mind was in a different place but I'd made a mistake that I had to correct. I spent a lot of time with my son and his mom. I also spent time with Kimmie.

When I went and paid my lawyer, he informed me that he could get me two years for everything but that I couldn't escape jail time. I couldn't understand doing time knowing that Gee Gee would admit that she had lied about her age and that her mom was aware we were having sex. My mind was set on probation or a trial.

Spring came and I was feeling more and more stressed, especially when Ria told me that she was pregnant again. I was fighting three cases and since I didn't have the dope houses anymore, my money wasn't as long, but I continued to hustle and kept the faith.

One day in May, Steph called and told me that I had to take the deal or go to trial. I had enough money to pay Steph, go broke and still go to jail, or I could go on the run and start flipping my cash until it was time for trial. I didn't want to go on the run with a newborn and a child on the way and on top of all that, my aunt had signed for me to bond out, so she would lose her house and her new Expedition if I ran. However, I couldn't imagine going back to jail. I had just done three years. It was the beginning of summer. I wasn't a rapist and I believed in my story. So, I ran!

25

Except for the previous summer when I visited my family in Minnesota, I had never been out of the state before. Martin's' sister Dominique had a friend that lived in Buffalo, New York and from listening and watching TV, I knew if I ever had to go on the run I would leave the state. So, Dominique called her friend Tyrica and we went to Buffalo. Martin offered to keep me company while I ran and I was grateful. Kimmie drove us to Buffalo in her brand new Honda Accord. Kimmie was smarter and more successful than any female we grew up with and she was loyal to me. More loyal than my own family.

Sometimes I took advantage of Kimmie. She was family in my mind. I would kill or die for her. We always had great conversation and great sex. It was always fun. I could be myself around Kimmie. She would talk about my crooked teeth and we cracked on each other's childhood traumas. We told each other our deepest secrets and we confided in each other. Kimmie was more loyal to me than all the fellas and twice as clever. Sometimes it seemed as if she was reading my mind. We were twenty-two years old, but we had known each other since we were eight.

On the way to Buffalo, I didn't know what to expect. I was very ignorant and fearless. The movie, "Belly" had just been released and I was on my "Tommy Buns" shit. But this was real life and Martin was with me no matter what. He didn't agree with everything I said. We would argue later, but at the time he had my back.

We arrived in Buffalo with nearly five ounces of dope. We met Tyrica and her husband Kelton. Tyrica was fine. She was real thick and brown skin. She probably stood about 5'4". She had a round ass and a flat stomach, but she didn't look like the most well-kept female. But she would do. Kelton was about 6'7". He had several brothers and they called them the Brolly Killers. His last name was Brolly and all his brothers were 6'5"or better, and raw. Kelton was dark skin with the deepest New York accent. I could barely understand him or their lingo. I introduced myself as Carl. Dominique had already told her friend that my name was Carl, so, Carl it was.

The first day in New York, Kelton took us to his block. It was called, "Monroe." He introduced us to E1, Lovie, Shoes and Dark. There were many others but those were the guys that we hung out with the most. E1 was a real handsome light skin kid, slim and about my height. Lovie was my skin color around 5'10 with a fit build. He was clean cut as well. Lovie and E1 were both around my age, both wore bulletproof vests every day and they argued constantly over who had the most bodies. They were two young hotheads like myself.

Shoes and Dark were Kelton's age and they were both polished and more reserved. . Shoes was dark skin with a football build. He was ugly with big lips. But he was cool. Dark was a little chunky and he was the man out the whole crew. They all welcomed us with open arms. Every day was hot as hell! The temperature seemed to always be 100 degrees or better. But, Buffalo, New York was the new home. I had to adapt to their temps and their hustle.

We were welcomed to hustle on Monroe, but I wanted my own territory, even out of state. I watched the Monroe Boys, the Camp Boys and Broadway Boys. In order to take over some territory, I had to know what I was in for on Monroe (or wherever we had to start hustling). Without an army, just Martin and a 38 Special. I had everything planned out. I would hustle and re-up with Dark, or do small re-ups from Shoes.

To extend gratitude, Dark gave me seven grams to start my hustle. They knew me as Carlton with no drugs or gun from another city. I thanked him. The street we stayed on was off of Broadway, but about two miles from Monroe. The guys in this area looked much weaker than the boys from that end of Broadway.

There was a small street called "Empire" that we walked past every day and it looked like these boys were booming. They weren't booming like Monroe, but they were making money. I told Martin that next time we walked to the store I would pull tight on these guys. Martin was with it. In the meantime we ate tuna and crackers every night and did push-ups. Kelton was usually gone and we were there with Tyrica. It was boring at best. Every time I thought of going home I knew I couldn't. Some days Tyrica would flirt with me but I never took the bait. I liked Kelton and he was our key to making it in Buffalo.

One night Kelton's friend came over around 2 am while Kelton was in the county for a small drug case. In fact, every night that Kelton was gone his friend came over. Martin and I ignored it but Tyrica could sense our discomfort. She preached about how our loyalty should be to her and she was right, so we continued to ignore his visits.

One morning we were walking to the store and we ran into a short fat guy that I had seen regularly on Empire. We approached him and I began to tell him that we were from Ohio and we wanted in on their little operation. I stared him in the eyes and talked firmly. I'm sure he was intimidated by the constant inconsistency in his eye contact. He was a coward. He told us we were welcomed to hustle there anytime, and we did. We walked the area daily. We would make a hundred dollars or two on Monroe and a few on Empire, just by walking. It was slow but we maintained.

After about thirty days, Tyrica and I started arguing all the time about money and other small issues. I actually think it was due to me not falling for her advances. One day I called my cousins in Minnesota. The whole family was aware of my situation. The police and bounty hunters had hit everybody's house in Cleveland with my last name. My cousins up north were anxious for me to get there so Kimmie drove to Buffalo to pick up me and Martin, but before I left Buffalo I had one last mission. I rode to Monroe to farewell them boys and I told Kelton about Tyrica fucking with his dude behind his back. I could tell he was hurt. All the Monroe boys looked sad. They told me I was welcome any time. They showed me a lot of love while I was there. My first week there we went to a Memphis Bleek concert and we partied every weekend free of charge. To Cleveland we drove. Martin went home and I went to a hotel. I gathered up the gossip and snuck to my granny's through the back door. She cried so hard. She said the police and bounty hunters were at her house every day. I was no doubt a ruthless villain, but my granny could always break me down. I hated that I had always been a disappointment to her. She told me to keep running if I thought I was innocent. I snuck to Ria's to see the baby, then called my cousins up north Mooki and Face had moved up to Minnesota.

My cousin Ricko, who was my mom's age had moved to Minnesota in the late 80s and made it sweet up there for everyone to come. All my cousins stayed in one of his houses. So I knew I would have somewhere to live. I went to Tito and grabbed some dope and two days later I was on the Greyhound to Minnesota. I hated leaving Ria four months pregnant, but I had no choice. Martin and I took the eighteen hour bus ride with the gun and drugs. When I arrived my whole family greeted me with open arms. I hadn't seen them in a year, but this time the situation was different. I would be staying for good or until I could buy my case. I was ready. I felt at home as soon as I got there. St. Paul is where I arrived.

26

Like anywhere else as soon as I arrived, I was looking for the money. I would be staying with my cousin Mooki and his girlfriend Sonya. Sonya was cold, brown skin with a cold ass body with big bright eyes and she was tall. She had three children, one of them was my one year old cousin. Including Martin and I, the house was packed. Sonya had a bad ass friend who came over daily. I forgot her name. They were both a few years older than I. Mooki had a Bronco, a Chevy and a small foreign car, so I always had something to drive.

My cousins Marco and Martin were there. They were two gigantic brothers. My cousin Armon was only nineteen and the whole city knew him due to him being a local high school football star. My cousin Face was Mooki's brother. We started to have fun as soon as I arrived. Marco was waiting to start back at the community college. All he talked about was girls. All I talked about was money. Mooki gave me tours every day and showed me where I could make the most money and what areas were supposed to be rough. Compared to Cleveland Minnesota was far less rough, so I felt comfortable and I began to hustle instantly.

I learned that University Avenue basically ran through the entire St. Paul area and up further was Frogtown, a neighborhood in St. Paul where you could find a lot of Chinese. The same way that the Arabs had monopolized Cleveland's street corner businesses, was the same way the Asians had done to St. Paul's businesses. Frogtown was a heavy drug area supposedly controlled by Asians.

I purchased a mountain bike and began to patrol the area. If I was out hustling, Martin would ride the bike and hustle also. But we were usually together. We quickly learned St. Paul and migrated to Minneapolis. We went wherever they said the money was. We wore flashy Coogi sweaters and colorful wave caps. Our swag was ten years ahead of them. They were clean, but in every city the ballers have a different dress code and swag. In Minneapolis, the streets that were pumping were 10th thru 20th, but it didn't seem sweet like Buffalo. I don't think my rugged approach would have worked. Martin and I had started wrapping our rocks individually in plastic and serving them out of our mouths. The money in Minnesota was coming way faster than Cleveland. A $20 rock in Cleveland was a $50 piece up there.

Instead of my tough approach I jumped out on 10th and asked the guys could they help me get some pills off. These boys weren't soft, they were just friendly and they showed us how to move in Minneapolis. Everything went smooth every day. I soon sent for Larry and Elmar. They didn't stay long enough to make money. But we had fun for a week until they got homesick.

The first week of school for Marco, I decided to go to school with him, just to visit and see the females. I hadn't had any pussy in weeks. I figured if I was going to be here I would need a girl. Martin had decided to go back home in a few weeks. I was going with him but just to re-up. The day I went to school with Marco I met a female name Sandra. She was fine as hell. She had the biggest face in the world with and hour glass shape. She was about 5' 5" and 140 pounds.

She was light brown skin complexion and she had a big nose.

If nothing else when you're on the run all you do is think. To Martin this was just an adventure because his record was clean. All that played in my head was the sound of the older guys in jail saying, "Youngsta you got another bid in you." I think what hurt the most was that I finally had this next level hustle down, but instead of hustling to get on, I was hustling to survive and pay lawyers. I still had to go to jail no matter what. I was on borrowed time, but one thing my grandmother always told me was, "Don't cry about nothing you can't fix. Just keep it moving and figure it out," so I hustled in Minnesota and squeezed some fun in from time to time.

I never showed my feelings. I kept a smile no matter what. I always felt I was stronger than those around me. No matter my situation I was always able to keep my mind focused on the task. Being on the run was building a fire inside of me and I knew if I was blessed enough to make it out of this situation I would make money and lots of it. All I did was think, think, think, and do push-ups. Every time I called home I heard different gossip; People were laughing at me or my family had turned against me.

One day my cousin Mooki put his mom Bell on the phone. She was also my grandmother's youngest sister and my favorite aunt besides Gale. When I was little she would pick me up and her sons Mooki and Face were my favorite older cousins. When I grabbed the phone from Mooki I was happy because I was sure Bell wanted to give words of encouragement. Her first words were loud and clear, "Take that shit to your people not to mine." I was crushed. She said it like I wasn't her nephew. She treated me like a stranger. I didn't say anything. I just gave Mooki the phone back. Most things that people were saying and doing to me, I knew I couldn't change their opinion, but I was glad I knew how they felt. I was truly the underdog. Some days I wanted to quit, but I knew I couldn't. I had kids to leave money behind for and a lawyer to pay. But fuck all that, first and foremost, I was a true champion in my mind. I would die before I quit. Martin and I began to hit small robberies at local bars on guys we knew were hustling or had won gambling. Never anything major, just a few hundred to add to the hustle money.

I went to visit Sandra in Minneapolis. She stayed on 1st Avenue South. Sometimes, I would go there just to get away. Sandra was from Mississippi and her family thought that my name was Carl. Her mom was Annie. She was the nicest southern woman in the world. Sandra had six brothers. All of them were at least 6' tall, all light brown skin with big hands and feet. They all had crazy southern accents. They seemed friendly but three of them were stone criminals. They actually all looked exactly like their father but they didn't deal with him because he had sexually assaulted Sandra years before. Sandra helped lighten my load of being on the run, when it seemed I didn't have a friend in the world.

In mid-September, Martin and I went back home. He was staying, but I was going to re up. I figured I would stay at Larry's. He still stayed on Mt. Auburn in Section Three but it was far enough away that I thought they wouldn't look for me on this end of 93rd. Kimmie would sneak over and I would only talk to my kids mom on the phone.

The first morning that I returned to Cleveland around 5:30 am I heard a lot of banging on Larry's door. Martin and I were in the living room. Then we heard bullhorns. We knew who it was and we knew it was over. My brain went into over drive. We woke Larry up as I laid on the floor military style. I ordered Larry and Martin to stand up and open the door in three minutes so I'd have time to crawl to the back of the house, flat on my belly. I made it to the kitchen with flashlights coming into every room. Larry ran past me to the back door and held it as the cops tried to barge in and that was all I needed. I ran all the way up to the third floor attic and put piles of clothing on top of me that Larry's dogs had pissed and shitted all over. Piles and piles and piles of pissy, shitty clothes. I could hear the police inside all over the house. It sounded like thousands of them. I was gasping for air but I wouldn't dare move. The smell was unbearable. I heard the police come to the third floor. I stopped breathing. They were knocking everything down and kicking things around. I remember feeling heavy objects land on top of me. I didn't know where they were but I wouldn't dare make a sound. I knew they were going to find me but this was my last attempt to stay free. I had nothing to lose. I heard the CB say, "all clear up here," but I thought it was a trick. I heard footsteps going down stairs, but I continued to lay upstairs for hours. I never moved. Then I heard music playing really loud so I went down stairs.

Kimmie and all the fellas were still downstairs. When they saw me everybody acted like they saw a ghost. Larry and his mom were saying, "Where the fuck were you? We thought you jumped out the window." They said that the police had tortured everyone but still they all said that they hadn't seen me. The police knew I was in town they said, even though I had only been in town twelve hours.

As soon as I got my composure everyone broke the news that Ria was in labor with my second child. But how could this be? She wasn't due until December. I went to the side of Larry's house with all my things and got into the trunk of Kimmie's Honda with her cellular phone and directed her through the folded down back seats. My Aunt Gale had heard the news. Kimmie took me to Gale.

I transferred my things to Gale's truck and laid in the back and off to Fairview Hospital we went. My aunt and I talked the whole way there as she cried crocodile tears. She said, "Chris, they want you dead or alive you're all over the posters and on the news." In my mind, I had tricked myself to think everybody was against me. So I'm thinking my aunt's tears weren't real and that she just wanted me to turn myself in so the bonds company wouldn't take her truck or her house. As I was getting out of her car at the hospital and thanking her for the ride, in my head I was thinking, "Wow, my aunt feels the same way everyone else does." She looked me in my eyes. It felt like we were in the house on Gibson and every word came out her mouth poetically, "Keep running if that's what you want to do. I can get this shit back." I cried on my way into the hospital. At that moment I knew what Tug meant when he preached, "Real family means everything."

When I asked what floor Ria was on I was nervous. They told me I would have to put on a mask and hospital shoes. I was thinking, "A mask? Thank God." When I arrived at the room she was on the table and her mom was in the room. They were explaining that I had given her Trichomoniasis and all types of other bacteria and that the baby would have complications. They also said that he had to be out of her body right now. The doctor was pulling green puss out of her and it looked nasty. I was ashamed and embarrassed. Ria pushed and a baby boy popped out, weighing only two 2 pounds. I was happy to see him born. I named him Love, after my dude in Buffalo. I had told him that I had a son on the way and that I would name him after him, because I liked his name. Leaving the hospital I found out Marty had been killed during a drug deal.

I went to the neighborhood. Everybody was hurt about Marty's death. Most just because he was the plug. But I genuinely always liked him as a person. He was smooth with class. His cars and jewelry were elegant. His right hand man was his cousin, Bull, who was a big, muscular, dark skin dude who loved building race cars and he was Marty's muscle. Bull's little brother Rahid, was about my age, but really quiet. He was tall, dark skin like his brother, and wore his hair braided. He had a medium muscular build and would always end up in a fight with Ali every month. For what reason I never knew.

I couldn't attend Marty's funeral. I had to cop work and get back to Minnesota. I rode all the way to Minnesota listening to the radio and thinking. The Ruff Ryder's and Cash Money was the hottest music out. Jay Z was making noise as always. My new life was in Minnesota. Sandra had replaced Martin's company. We dated frequently and usually we would go see all the new movies; The Matrix, Life, etc. I always watched Belly and compared my situation to it. But I couldn't wake up and read a script of my own life. My story was real.

27

Now I was in Minnesota alone. I moved in with my cousin Armon, who partied every day and smoked his weed. He had a lot of friends. Armon was bi-racial. His dad, my cousin Ricko was dark skin and his mom was white. He had friends of both races. Every weekend Armon and I went to the hottest parties. He introduced me to his dad's property manager Ted, a fat white guy that wore glasses, who snorted coke and smoked crack. Yet Ted was cool because he spent lots of money. I could give him credit in huge amounts and he would always pay. Everything was going smooth. I had almost reached my goal.

Winter had arrived. In Minnesota the winter was ten times worse than in Cleveland. I had adapted to everything else but the weather. It hardly snowed but the wind would cut your breath off as well as the skin on your face. It was cold.

Sandra and I were having the best sex ever. She was a square or at least she acted like it. She said I was the first guy she ever gave head to. I would ask her daily and she would always deny me. Then one day she ask me, "Do you want me to bite it?" I said, "Yeah, go ahead." However I could get it in her mouth I would. She sucked my dick like a porn star. Slob and spit everywhere. She never used her hands and every day after that she swore I was the first. I didn't care. I was from 93rd. Every girl gave head by the age of 15.

I had a routine. When Armon went to work I got up to hustle. I did push-ups all day while I was home. I didn't think about home much or I tried not to. It hurt not being able to see my granny daily and my newborn sons, but I was safe and making money. Actually, I had become something that Tug told me to never ever become, and that was comfortable. I spent Thanksgiving in Minnesota. I had stopped driving all together. I caught the bus to Sandra's or rode with my cousins. I kept a low profile. One morning I called Larry and he said, "My nigga on the front page of the plain dealer." I asked, "for real?" He told me that I was wanted for distributing dangerous drugs across 93rd area.

That night my cousin Armon came in the house and said, "Uncle Carl and my grandma want to talk to you, but I don't think you should call." But I called anyway. I talked to Carl and Dora, my uncle and aunt for hours. Carl told me that I was living off my animal instinct and he tried to convince me to turn myself in but I refused. I hadn't known that there was a reward out for me until it was in the newspaper. I hung up the phone with Carl and Dora. Then Dora's son, Ricko called. He was also Armon's dad. Ricko was always down to earth, but when he called he told me to leave. I didn't understand why. But in so many words he told me that somebody was going to tell on me. That night Sandra begged me to come over. I told her I would be there first thing in the am. Armon and I had a heart to heart conversation. He told me he admired me and that I always seemed older than I was. Armon was weird but he did his own thing. I always could feel the love.

Early the next day, Armon went to work. I had a funny feeling and I looked outside. The whole house was surrounded by US Marshalls. They even had the stands for the guns mounted into the snow. They yelled my name out on bullhorns. "Christian Hayward come out. If you try to run we will shoot!" I could hear them in the house. I ran to the second floor from the third where Armon stayed and acted like I lived there. When they came to the second floor and asked my name I said, "Ant Kendrick." Then I gave them a fake ID stating that was my name. Even though they were federal agents they were confused. They rounded up every one in the house and asked them, "Where is Christian Hayward?" and everyone said the same thing, "That's our cousin in Cleveland."

After hours of me trying on clothing from the third floor and answering what seemed like hundreds of questions and just when I thought I had the Marshalls fooled, they called Cleveland Police. They called to ask if Ant Kendrick had tattoos and was told that he did not. Even though Ant had a clean police record, he was a known high school basketball star so they called South High School, when he attended and they faxed photos. The photo identities didn't match. I knew the gig was up. I was busted and believe it or not I felt relieved. I left all my money because it was in the same bag with my drugs. I put on my coat and left shackled. They strapped me in a van and one of the agents told me, "When you're on the run never trust anyone not even your family on the phone." At that moment I recollected all of the events from the past twenty-four hours, and I knew that it was Dora and Carl that set me up.

I arrived at Hennepin County Jail. I knew Cleveland had ten days to pick me up. It felt like life was over. Not because of the situation, but because I didn't know what to expect when I got back. I called my great-grandparents for my first call. My great-grandfather got on the phone and reminded me of a time I had broken my word to him, He said, "Last time we talked you broke your word to me. You'll probably never see me again. I'll be dead, but remember this, never break your word and never respect a man who does!" I was lost for words. But before I could respond my great grandmother was back on the phone. She wished me well and told me to stay strong.

I called Armon and everybody acted like the police had taken my money. I was defeated. Nine more days I would be back in Cleveland. A lot of Chicago guys migrate to Minnesota to get money. Half of Minnesota's County Jail was Chicago natives. I didn't talk much. Shit I didn't talk at all. Whenever anyone would ask me where I was from I would say Cleveland, and they would ask a million questions.

One day a guy name Crusher from Chicago asked me "Do u like "Do or Die" or "Twister?" I replied dryly that they were both okay rap artists. Then, he said, "I bet yo bitch ass like Bone." I was shocked. I hadn't been disrespected since I was a teen and everybody after that received a terrible ass whooping. I looked around. There was at the very least thirty guys watching. My respect meant everything no matter where I went. I said, "Please don't disrespect me" and he replied loudly, "What the fuck you gone do?" I don't think he was use to a challenge. I stood up to make sure he didn't get the ups. Several guys were saying, "Crusher, fuck him up."

Crusher was dark brown skin and a little taller than me, about my build. He looked like he lived a rough life. But honestly, I thought I could take him. I had seen his kind before. I knew I had no win in this county pod, but I wouldn't back down. I'd rather go down fighting. So we faced off. He said one thing and that's what I respected about him. He didn't do much talking. His only words were, "I'm 'bout to whoop your ass." As soon as he began to jump around I knew by the way he held his guards he couldn't fight very well. But I don't underestimate anybody. Before we could fight all the old heads broke it up. They were all saying, "Youngsta ain't no coward he's from the city of game." I had nothing to prove. I would never see these guys again.

That night my cellmate, one of Crusher's boys, spit on the cell floor and I beat him like a woman and he was at least 6' tall. He went out like a coward. He even stopped fighting back. I didn't sleep the rest of the night nor the next morning. I asked the CO to remove me from the pod and I was placed on the trustee pod away from all the gang bangers. I played ping pong all day. There I met Sleepy, an ugly, big lip guy around 6' 1" and light brown skin. He was cut up like a NFL player. Sleepy was back from prison trying to get an early release from a manslaughter charge and he had just got out from doing a murder. Everyone respected him. He had zero tolerance. I think he was a vice lord. He was a bad dude. He was from St. Louis, and he talked with a southern accent. We laughed and joked all day long.

Minnesota was different from Cleveland. The guys I met with manslaughters only did five and six years before they were back home with ten to twenty years of probation. It was sweet up there to me. I saw a guy from Chicago while in the county that I use to always see when I was hustling in St. Paul. He was moving packs like me. He would always try to hook-up but I refused. He drove a real nice Monte Carlo SS. He and Sleepy got into an argument over use of the phone.

The guy portrayed a rugged Chicago image on the street. He was as tall as Sleepy but not as built. He was black as hell and thick. Sleepy beat him like he stole his money. The guy couldn't fight at all. That was the last time I ever saw Sleepy.

The next day during arraignment I was placed in the bullpen with all the guys back from the penitentiary or awaiting court. One guy stood out because he was a gigantic white boy around 6' 6", all muscle. But what made him stand out is the fact that he was drawing and seemed to be really into it. A few minutes went by and a group of familiar faces came into the bullpen, including Crusher and a few of the guys from the pod I had left. All I could do was ask myself, "God why me?" I remained cool for about fifteen minutes. Then, they all began to heckle and whisper until Crusher and another guy jumped up saying they would beat my ass and send me back to Cleveland in a box, etc. My only option was to beat on the door and call for the CO but my body wouldn't let me. So I just looked at them as they proceeded to talk about me being a ho ass nigga, etc. They all said I was lying about being from Cleveland. Then out of nowhere the big white boy stood up and said, "Who wants to fight him?" Everyone was silent. Then he looked and asked me was I willing to fight a fair one. I replied, "Most definitely!" But nobody was willing to fight me one on one and I knew at that moment that they were cowards because one big man couldn't stop no show with me and my dudes back home. They all began to explain their reasons for not wanting to fight and mumbling under their breath as they sat down. I was called to see the judge and sent back to my pod.

The next morning was the tenth day and I rode out. Transportation arrived. I was twenty-three years old. I was on the road with guys younger than me being transferred, federally. They had photos with their Mercedes Benz, Lexus, Suburbans, and Vettes, etc. They reminded me that I was playing out there hustling in the streets. Even though these boys were from all over the U.S., they were thorough. There is no certain location that makes you thorough. I knew whenever I was released it was on. I arrived in the Cuyahoga County jail.

28

The only thing good about the county was constant visits and the fact that you knew everything was about to be over because I was actually tired of running. I was in the new county jail this trip, 11 A. I knew most of the people on the pod. Fat Wes from Miles, Trey and Neeka's brother Laneer my crew.

My cellmate, Catfish, had one eye and he gambled all day. Keshonte from Section Two was there as well. We were real close. Jason from Quincy. Trayvon from Miles and Lil Zack was there. Zack was my friend Silver's little cousin. Zack, a tall slim baby face kid was only eighteen and in for two murders. He looked harmful like Silver did when he went down for his murders at that age. I called them the killer cousins. Both Pie from Tarkington, and Isley from Buckeye had also came back from the joint.

Me and my cellmate hit it off swell, but his breath smelled worse than the toilet. He had two missing front teeth. He was light skin and my height and we were about the same build. Ironically, I thought he was cool and he tried me the next day. I was so frustrated from being locked up, I slammed him and just started choking him and he never tried me again. He pulled a pencil out on me afterward but I told him I would brutally beat him if he didn't put it away. As weeks went on we were cool.

Ria brought my boys to see me almost seemed like every day. I stayed on the phone and sometimes I gambled. It was hard adapting to this world again. Me and Laneer reminisced about two years prior when I had boxed Sajo at the gym. We had good laughs. Everybody around me knew I would possibly be taking the long ride but we never discussed time or charges.

Jason was my dude in juvenile years ago. He was a couple of years older than me and he hung with Pie and Isley on the pod. They were supposed to be tough guys, but I didn't care. I just watched them disrespect guys daily. Jason dogged my cellmate real bad one time. He lost gambling and chalked (refused to pay) him out loud in front of the whole pod. My cellmate cried actual tears. I secretly didn't like Jason after that anymore. I would never fight for a guy who wouldn't fight for himself. One day he and I were playing cards and he hinted that he might not pay me, which was awkward because Jason knew I didn't take any shit. He was a real stocky kid, very ugly, and much louder than he was tough. I told him that if he thought about not paying me it would be handled asap. He jumped up making a scene so I slapped him with the cards. We got up and squared off. All I remember is Fat Wes and Laneer saying, "Watch this y'all" to the pod. As soon as Jason threw his guards up I dropped him with the cleanest two piece ever thrown. He jump right back up like a cat. He was embarrassed. He couldn't fight. He rushed me with his head down. I knocked him all over the pod with punches. He never even hit me. While they were breaking it up and I was restrained, he broke loose and ran over and hit me in the eye and it swelled up pretty bad, but he was the loser so they removed him from the pod.

The next day Isley and Pie came to my cell admiring my fighting skills. I simply asked them, "Ain't Jason y'all dude?" They answered "yes" and my reply to them was, "No reason y'all should be talking to me. Leave my cell."

I never wanted to pat myself on the back, but I knew I was fearless. I was a real dog and as Ed Boom would call me, "A pretty dog." I was handsome with a young face. I was more like a myth because my stories didn't fit the way I look. Every time I met a new crew I could see the disbelief in their eyes. But I rarely got tried. The stories got bigger as they traveled. If I knocked one guy out. The streets said it was two. If I shot a guy the streets said I killed 'em. I had a reputation in the streets but it didn't mean anything in jail. Right after I beat up Jason my eye hadn't even went down before I got into another fight.

There was a guy on the pod that danced all day and we would all watch him just to kill time. Then one day the kid Trayvon from 119th and Miles said, "Sit your corny ass down." People rarely spoke up when Trayvon talked tough 'cause they were scared. That day I wanted to see if he was really that tough so I said, "I'm sure you're corny to somebody too." We locked eyes and before he could speak I hit him with everything I had. He stumbled and fell into his boys arms and when he got up his words were, "When you hit first you're supposed to knock the nigga out." I couldn't believe it. He took the mighty right hand and came back. We rumbled all over the pod. I don't know how we ended up on the floor but we did. We were on our knees going toe to toe blow for blow. Trayvon wasn't soft. He had the fight in him. I always rather fight a guy like that than a bitch ass nigga. I was impressed. They broke the fight up. We were both tired. I guess the CO considered him the loser or they didn't like him because I remained on the pod again. But I secretly respected Trayvon.

The county was all mental this time. Everybody in the county says that they're going to do things differently once they're released and that they learned their lesson, but I meant it. I was struggling financially. I had been hustling on the streets ten years without anything to show. I was the cause of my aunt losing everything she had. I was in the rear with the people that meant the most to me and it was just like Tug said, "When shit hit the fan all you'll have is your family."

It was the summer of 2000. I fought and fought and fought. I still lost my trial. When the jurors came back with the verdict I could have died, but I stayed strong for my family. I was sentenced to seven years at Lorain Correctional Facility. The judge told me that I wouldn't be getting out early. My whole neighborhood and everybody else I knew was there. My aunt spoke at my sentencing as well as all my dudes and their moms. But it didn't matter. The judge had her mind made up. She said I justified selling drugs like they were legal. The prosecutor said the streets praised me and my neighborhood idolized me. They made the case bigger than rape.

Even though I took the stand in my defense and even though Gee Gee testified on my behalf that I didn't know her age, the remains of the baby were tested and the baby was 99.9 percent mine. The state law is that no child under sixteen is within the legal age to consent to sex, so even without force the charge still would have been rape.

I wasn't labeled as a sexual predator, but a sexual orientated offender, meaning my face wouldn't be posted anywhere and I wouldn't have to register with the sheriffs for the rest of my life, but I felt like my family felt; Jail should have been the punishment for both me and Gee Gee's mom.

Sometimes I wish I would have went along with the extortion plot and gave her mom the $5000 she demanded in order to not press charges. My lawyer had informed me that even though her mom knew the whole situation and condoned it, that it wouldn't matter and that I would more than likely lose the trial. The jury still had to go by the law books.

I felt bad for Gee Gee because despite our age difference she was cool and I knew this ordeal would affect her for life. I considered the five years that I received for the rape case harsh, but I justified my punishment by thinking, "No 21 year old male with polish, would fuck a female under 18, regardless." So I accepted and took full responsibility for my actions.

Once I was sentenced I was relieved. I knew I would be in Lorain reception in a few days and wherever they sent me after that would be my parent institution. I couldn't imagine being thirty years old. I definitely couldn't imagine getting out of jail at thirty. But that was my reality. I can honestly say that I never thought about leaving the streets alone. I loved the streets. I began to think about every major player from 93rd. I knew nobody from my whole area had ever touched one million dollars cash at one time. At this point in my life all I wanted to do was conquer the game.

I was a sex offender. I had embarrassed myself and my family. I left my children out there without a father. I quickly grew a chip on my shoulder. My reputation had grew to be larger than life. I was only 5' 9" with the respect of a giant. I was rumored to have done a lot of people wrong.

In the streets if you shoot at people you're a gangsta. If you kill one person you're a killer. If you can fight well you're a knockout artist. But my thoughts at this time were, "I have nothing to show for any of the things I've done." At one point you become ashamed. I knew my seven years would do one or two things; it would sharpen me up or weaken me. In my mind, I would have wasted thirty years of my life. I had no more games to play and too much to prove.

When I went to my cell after sentencing, I walked back to the pod. Everyone had already heard the news. It was silent when I walked through the door. I smiled to keep from crying. I entered my cell and my cellmate at the time was Crazy Legs Tim Melton, a white boy from Broadway. He was back from the joint for judicial release. He wasn't your typical weak white boy. Tim was 6'4" and he was tough. He asked me, "Did they really give you seven years?" I responded, "Yes" but he expected me to be upset. When actually, I was waiting to ride out in three days. Tim and I said our farewells and promised to stay in contact. He had received his judicial a few days before my sentencing.

29

I was shipped to Lorain. This time it was a little different. I had children and I couldn't get past what I was locked up for and the fact that I had basically been selling drugs my whole life and came to jail broke. Again, I remembered guys telling me my first bid, "Youngsta you got another bid in you." I thought they were all haters. As soon as I got to Lorain I saw Cal Sims, a short dark skin kid from Kinsman. Sims had an older brother Fred Sims. They looked identical, but Fred was tall. I'd known them both my whole life. They both could box and had a lot of respect on the streets. Cal was a year older than me and my height and all the girls liked him. He always had nice cars and jewelry. Everybody liked the Sims' brothers. They always smiled, but you knew they meant business.

I wasn't doing too well financially in Lorain and Cal carried me the whole month that I was there. My kids mom ironically lost touch as soon as I left the county. No calls or letters. No word on my appeal. I literally went through Lorain for a month without going to the store. Cal gave me $10 a week and he never asked for anything back. We never hung out on the streets but the respect was always there. He was a little more advanced than me. He was doing what the older guys were doing. He even had grown women for girlfriends. I gained a new respect for Cal and I promised myself one day I would show him how appreciative I was for his help. Lorain was a blur. I was twenty-three years old and my hairline got thin. I hadn't done anything significant on the streets. I had no college degree and I had disappointed my grandmother. But I refused to keep beating myself up.

I was finally transferred to Mansfield Correctional Institution. This was the prison of all prisons for the boys up north. I was nervous. This was where I would spend my next six and a half years. I kept remembering the judge say, "No early release." They gave me a tan jumpsuit (monkey suit) that everyone wears their first three days until issued your blues, then they pointed to my block and said, "Hayward, you're going to 2-B." It seemed like a mile away. I rode in with a bunch of people who all seemed scared. But I knew I would be cool. One, because I wasn't takin no shit from nobody and two, because I knew I would know everyone. I walked down the sidewalks of the clean brown brick college-like atmosphere with manicured lawns until I reached 2-B. Each block had four pods; 1 thru 4, A-D.

As soon as I was buzzed in I talked to the CO and they told me where my cell was. I heard my name being called from everywhere and I saw a lot of familiar faces. D-Bay, Tyson, Doe-Boy, and a lot of guys I hadn't seen in ten years. I hadn't seen any of these guys since we were teens. They had all been down ever since and even though these were terrible circumstances they were more than happy to see me. They all gave me big care packages with food and hygiene. They all wanted to hear stories about the streets. They all had been down since at least 1994 and had at least five or ten years left on their sentences.

Mansfield was close security. You had to have close to ten years or better to go there. It was mostly murderers, rapist and robbers housed there. The worst of the worse. It was exactly like you see on the movies. Homos were everywhere. Guys kissing each other and holding hands and actually fighting over these chumps. I couldn't understand. I didn't even look at homosexuals as human beings. Zig was on the pod as well. I knew him from the projects that my mom stayed in. He had been down since 1992 or 1993. He was tall and dark skin, and had a muscular build. He was real smooth, always joking and laid back. Everyone liked Zig. He and his co-defendant were rumored to have been teen hit men with multiple bodies. Neither of them told on each other, and Zig had a few life sentences but you couldn't tell by his attitude. His co-defendant was Mall. I had never met him. I only heard the stories.

I quickly adapted to the ways of the joint. My hairline seemed to be getting worse as the days went on, so D-Bay gave me an M1 (bald head). I was only twenty-three, but I liked the clean look so I stuck with it. I started a store as soon as I got there. My kids' mom was still MIA. My granny sent me some money and Sammy sent me a startup kit of $500, so I was good. I ordered my TV and shoes and began to bid.

Next door was Crab's son Martin. Of all his sons, Martin and I were the closest. He had eight years for robberies. We talked every day. One day he came outside and told me that he had some bad news. I couldn't imagine what it was. It was a hot summer day in August. He told me that he called home and found out that my kid's mom was fuckin one of my best friends, Snake. I acted as if I wasn't hurt, but my legs were weak. My body was paralyzed. This was only supposed to happen in the movies or in a Triple Crown book. Not to Christian. All I kept thinking was, "This has to be a rumor." But it explained the two months, with no contact. I called home that night. She accepted my call. I was shocked. She acted real happy to hear from me. I couldn't say anything but, "Why Snake." She act as if she didn't know what I was talking about, so I just stayed silent. She began to cry and say it was only one time and she would never do it again. Then, I called Snake and he acted as if nothing had happened and greeted me like normal. He had actually just sent some photos of his new Cadillac on 20" wheels. Red was both of our favorite color. We did everything together every day while I was out. We slept in the same fien cars and same bed in crack houses all night hustling. Snake's mom Dell was like my own mom. She got high, and even though Snake served her I didn't care if she had $100, I refused to serve her. I asked him why he fucked my baby mama, but he had no explanation worth listening to. I hung up on them both. Even though I knew I would need them both, my pride wouldn't let me continue either relationship. I knew that day I would have a long bid.

I walked the track daily with D-Bay and Shorty Hough. Shorty Hough was D-Bay's homie. His name came from his height and where he was from. He was about 5' 6" and real cocky. He was a shade darker than me, a country sounding nigga that always seemed mad and ready to whoop somebody's ass. He had killed somebody and been down since he was fifteen years old. Shorty seemed like a dog and his reputation was such, but I wasn't one to quickly believe in reputations. Word on the compound was that Cee Black was the absolute pound for pound champ in Mansfield. I could believe it from being locked up with him in Marion years ago. I always remembered him getting Roy Starks off me and basically saving me when my own homies didn't. Cee Black was happy to see me. They said Cee Black had whooped every tough nigga worth whooping. He feared nobody; big, tall, or small. He was puttin in work. He wasn't on my pod. Mansfield was split up into two sides. If you were on the north side you might not see somebody on the south side for months, unless y'all met at the Rec gate and their pod had rec at the same time as yours. Unit One went to rec with Unit Three and Unit Two went with Unit Four.

I had homies all over the joint and the word was out. Everyone knew Chris was a dog, so I wasn't expecting any problems. But I thought to myself, "If Cee Black and Peanut had to fight I'm sure my day would arrive." Mansfield was wild. You were either predator or prey. Wasn't no in between. You had the Old School Booty Bandit Killers who had been down since the 70s. You had the Muslims. You had the Arian Brotherhood white boys and the young strong black dudes who just stayed in the mix. Then you had prey. The guys who gambled all day and lost constantly and stayed owing. You had the homos who I hate to admit stayed living large one way or the other. You had the young weak dudes who had to pay to stay alive and you had the old guys who were cool and just kept to themselves and everyone left them alone. It was balance in the joint and everyone knew their place.

I ran my store and played ping pong all day against Peanut, Chief, and Burt. Chief was a cool kid from Chicago. Burt was a slick talking nigga from Cleveland, always joking around. He was tall and slim, but cut-up nicely due to the fact he had been down ten years for a murder. All of his co-defendants were in Mansfield, but I'd only met Goody. I didn't know the others. I was also cool with the other Burt as well, from Chicago. Burt had twenty years for getting caught with thirty kilos. I would listen to his stories all the time and I just knew he was lying. He showed photos and I still didn't believe. I would think, "Who really has five and six hundred thousand dollars and travelled like this. I knew Golden and Sammy and Tito. But I don't think even they had the type of money this guy talked about. Even though he seemed to be lying. I still dreamed of living that life one day. Burt was dark skin, laid back, about 6 feet and stocky. Every tooth in his mouth was gold. Every story he told involved at least 100k and his brother Kerme. Burt sounded real country to me. But I had heard that accent before while living in Minnesota from the Chicago boys that lived up there.

The daily routine of Mansfield was actually not bad. Making the best of the situation was easy because there was always something going on. There was a lot of trading, gambling, and dealing all day. As I began to maneuver around I started to see more and more familiar faces. But I was happiest to see D-Rock, Silver, and Robert Dixon. They all were childhood friends that I had pretty much known my whole life. I hadn't seen D-Rock or Silver since I was a teen. All three of them had murder cases. D-Rock still looked the same except he was about 6 feet tall now, built like a boxer, and muscular with very broad shoulders. Even though his situation was what it was he still maintained his macho, I can't lose attitude. Rob was even taller than he was as a child but he was slim and very muscular. Both Rob and Silver were Muslim now. Silver was a fat kid but he had built his body into muscle over the years while he was locked up. He still didn't talk much and he had a very serious attitude. All three of them had the same thing in common. They were vicious and none of them believed their enemies should walk the earth. Shit if you wasn't with our squad they believed you shouldn't be breathing. They all loved Chris and were loyal to me and I felt the same.

Most of the guys I hung around with in Mansfield I already knew, except one kid from Cedar. He would always look at me but not with aggression. It was almost as if he was trying to figure me out as I talked that big shit. I knew who he was. His name was Freddie but they called him Flex. He was about my height which was 5' 9" at the time. He had hazel eyes and he was a very light brown complexion with a very large nose and very curly hair. Everyone knew him because he was one of the first and the youngest kids in the state of Ohio to be bound over to the adult system. He was fifteen when he had killed someone. And he had by far the best physique in the institution due to his dedication to working out. He even had the legs to match. He would work out and everyone would watch in awe like he was training for a professional fight. And Big Davar was from Kinsman where Sammy, Black Dre and Boots were from. He was about 6'1" and 270 lbs of muscle. He was almost as built as Flex, but much bigger. Var and I had also known each other our whole life or since we were boys. He had earned a terrible reputation in the streets for robbing anybody and not caring about the consequences later. But Var wasn't anything to play with. He was the epitome of a live wired hot head with the capability to handle a few guys at once. I wasn't too familiar with Freddie. I just admired his workout and his body. We would nod in respect but that's it.

One day out of the clear blue I was transferred to the whole opposite side of the joint. I didn't know why. I hadn't been in any trouble or fights. I was pissed. They moved me from the wildest pod on the north side to the church pod on the south side 3-A. I went thru the door going wild. It was so quiet you could hear a mouse take one step. When I walked thru the door everybody began to stare. I looked for young faces but there were none. Except for Goody and Flex. They seemed to be pretty close. Goody was Burt's co-defendant. He was about 5' 10" and built like an NFL Linebacker just real stocky and not too much fat. He was dark skin with the thick old man mustache with a perfect smile. He approached me with a very positive attitude and said, "Youngsta relax, it ain't that bad over here." He was around twenty-eight at the time. He help me situate my things in my cell and told me the rules of that pod. I knew I would hate the pod. My celly was an older man name Spence. Spence was around 5' 9" real slim a dark brown skin guy with normal features. I observed the smell of smoke when I entered the cell. I was even more pissed. All I could think about was "no fun". No fun meant time went slow. But I always remembered Tug saying, "I real player can adapt anywhere and make it work for him." And my whole life I was always great at adjusting because my granny always preached, "Crying don't change shit the problem will still be there." When they locked my cell for count it felt like my whole bid had started over again. It was Spring 2001.

30

Every day I would go to the gate to meet the guys on the north side where I had just left and me and Spence had begun to talk. And I met Tre Hendrick from East Cleveland. Tre was probably twenty-seven. I wasn't sure 'cause he always lied about his age. He was about 5' 10" and a little darker than me with a million dollar smile. He was cocky and every one respected Tre. They respected him a lot. Crab's son Martin had introduced us thru the fence a few months prior but now we were on the south side together. I was adjusting. I would leave out the pod and meet Tre or Var. Or I would stay on the pod with Goody and Flex. In about two months time me and Flex had built and inseparable bond. I loved flex like family. He still had the innocents of a kid. But he was a criminal to the core. And that's all we talked about. Robberies and drugs. Even though Flex had been locked up since 1990 he still read books and kept up with technology. All I talked about was a Mercedes Benz and making a million, I didn't care how I had to do it. Outside the pod Tre would talk about starting his own wine company and opening a club called the OH-10. Everybody around me were big dreamers. Time on what I considered The Church Pod had began to fly.

It was the end of 2001. I had begun to workout daily with Flex and Goody. Goody was very positive and it had started to rub off on me. I changed my diet. I began to read a lot and just relax. There were no young guys on my pod. None of the violence went on. So I was able to do a lot of thinking. I had accepted my situation. I only had five more years I had never been in a fight. I thought everything was cool. One day an older guy on the pod named Mr. Jay walked over to me and said "I watch you all the time youngsta you got a crown on and don't even know it. " he told me I reminded him of himself when he was young. Mr. Jay was probably 6' 3" real handsome bald head guy brown skin. Real smooth skin and he would always speak to me. He always had a different book in his hand. Then one day he came to my cell and gave me a book and told me to read it. When I looked down at the book he said, "Don't let nobody read this book." He said, "It ain't for everybody." I looked down and the cover said "The 48 Laws Of Power". I thought, "What the fuck is this about?" I had nothing else to do so I began to read it. I read it all night and I couldn't put it down. It was the best two or three chapters I had ever read.

I woke up the next day to Flex opening my cell before breakfast. He had a sad look on his face. He told me that a year ago he had put in a transfer request to Lake Erie Correctional when his security status dropped and that he was leaving after breakfast. We had been together every day for about eight months. Right before we walked out the door Mr. Jay approached me with a small piece of paper and ask me, "Did u like the book" I smile and said, "Yeah so far." Then he handed me a little piece of paper and said, "This is how you get your own go get my book." On the paper was the order form for the book. I said, "Give me a few more days." He replied, "You'll respect it more if you get your own." I gave him the book and walked to breakfast with Flex.

Mansfield was different without Flex. I rarely called home. But this weekend would be my first visit. I found out that I had lost my first step of my appeal process so had got a tattoo covering my entire back that said FUCK THE LAW and I meant it from the heart. I was down but not out. Regardless of the fact, I had five years to go. The guys around me would never see daylight again. The older guys like Glyn Bob, Ronald Ray, Simon, etc., would always remind me that my time was nothing and that I would be young when I got out. My friend Shontel had gotten in touch with me as well as Kimmie. They would both visit me and send money regularly.

The only thing that really mattered was receiving a visit this weekend from my boys. I hadn't seen Chrishon or Love since county and that was about fourteen months ago. I was excited and I promised that even though my kids' mom messed around with my best friend I would act polished and not mention the situation. Before the visit I decided to go workout with Var and Peanut. We were doing the usual, push-ups and pull-ups while waiting on me to be called to my visit. It was a warm Saturday morning. Everybody was under the shack. Me, Dee Dee, and Var would do pull-ups in sets of five until somebody quit. I'm talking nonstop. Sometimes we would get to thirty or forty sets. Even though it was only five pull-ups it was serious and we would all die before quitting.

During our work out a guy named Tot from the projects began to circle around me and out of the blue for no reason, he says "You a lil nigga." I really didn't know Tot. I would just see him on the yard along with the other project boys. I didn't know his motive I just wanted my visit, so I kept doing pull ups. But at this time every one seen his body language and began to crowd around. He kept saying things that insinuated that I wasn't tough as everyone thought or the rumors that he had heard. He had actually began to cross the line of respect to disrespect. The more I didn't argue. The more he talked. Dee Dee, Peanut and Var were all surprised that I let him talk that much, but at the time seeing my children were more important. Then Peanut told the crowd, "I know Chris and Tot can't beat him." But you could see that the whole Rec yard was in doubt of my skills. So I said, "My man I just want to see my children and once I'm back we can fight all day." Respect meant everything in the joint. One sign of weakness and it's over. I knew today was that day. I had promised myself if he said another word I would devour him. And at that moment Var said, "Chris, you have to dog him and say fuck everything." I knew my respect was on the line. Tot was about my height and light skin. He was a little thicker than me and built because he had been locked up for about four years. He looked hard but my past experiences wouldn't let me believe he or any man could beat me. He shouted out, "Fuck yo visit and yo kids."

It seemed like the yard went silent. I was speechless. In a very low tone I said, "Are u really that hard my nigga," but I was approaching him as I said it. Before he could even respond I had spit toward his face and before the spit hit his face I had hit him with the prettiest right hand ever and he hit the ground. I was furious now. Everybody that knew me was laughing loud as could be and all the project boys were helping Tot up. He began to ask for better shoes to fight with and I promised the crowd that whoever gave him the shoes would be next. Nobody even attempted to give him tennis shoes. Then I heard, "HAYWARD" and I looked back it was the officer calling me "HAYWARD 389253!!" I said, "Yes". He said, "Visit," I left the Rec yard still trembling from adrenaline.

31

I saw my boys for the first time in over a year. I was nervous because of the fear of them not knowing me. But to my surprise they both came straight to me like they had been around me. It was weird. It was more awkward meeting up with my children's mom after she had done what she did the previous year with Snake. I still wasn't over it. I don't know if it was because I loved her or if it was just my ego. Whatever the situation was it still hurt when I thought about it. But despite all of that we still had a great time. We reminisced and she told me several times how clear my skin was and I looked in shape. My sons were about two and almost three years old. Every time I looked at them I thought about the facts that I never had a mom or dad and I was repeating the cycle. Once the visit was over I went back to my cell and shed a few tears.

Tug always came to visit me. Even if he was going thru one of his spells of getting high. He still came at least once every other month. He still sent money and food boxes. He was always everything to me since I was a baby and he continued no matter my situation. I loved Tug to death and I knew nothing would ever come between us. I knew I had to do better when I was released. I knew I had a point to prove. I knew it was bigger than Christian Hayward. Now I knew what Tug meant when he said, "Whatever you do be the best at it."

2018

THE STREET GOD II
"The Rise Of A Legend"

Christian Hayward

A Saturday night. sitting at the Sunoco Gas Station, in a snow blizzard with a flat tire, out of gas, without a dollar in my pocket. I looked across the street at the car wash that I had previously owned for the past three years. But I had just lost it, along with my 2008 Tahoe, 2005 BMW and my 2005 Honda Accord, as well as a few properties. Now, I was driving around in a 1990 Honda, a stick shift. I had fell from Grace.

I was riding around daily doing small robberies with Black Jo. He was one of the young guys from my neighborhood and also one of the most ruthless individuals from UTW. I considered myself ruthless, but I wasn't 10% as heartless as Black. The one thing that we had in common was our loyalty for the game and towards each other.

Black was Sal's little cousin. He was 6' and 250 lbs., all muscle and he was a lot like Sal. They were both able to destroy you without a weapon. I loved Black. Some days he would hit licks and give me half of the money even if I wasn't with him. I told him daily I would bounce back and he always believed in me. We suffered together daily, as well as watched each other's back.

I was in a daze as my cousin Jamell pulled up. I was relieved, thinking, "Finally. I can get some gas and put air in my tire." I was freezing cold. Jamell pulled out a big knot of cash and bragged about having a car full of chicks, as he pumped gas into his own car. I explained to him my situation and asked him for $20. He looked at my car and said, "I can't do it. I have something to do with this." He jumped back into his 2006 Charger and pulled off with the females as if I wasn't standing there in the cold. It was almost as if that was the win he always wanted over me. Jamell was just like his dad, so I wouldn't dare ask him a second time. I would have rather died than beg him. I knew I had put myself in this position. I had been out of prison longer than I ever had before (four years). I went through millions of dollars, hit gigantic robberies and I had made six figures off of every narcotic and I was broke with nothing, sitting here at the mercy of peasants.

I called one of my older dudes, Coot. He was a true O.G from 131st. I already owed Coot $10,000 for money he let me borrow a few months prior, but he still came through. He came to the gas station, lectured me as usual and then gave me a $100 bill. I bought a Hershey with almonds, got some gas, and put air in my tire.

Even though I was in the streets, believe it or not, I was still a member of the Word Church. Pastor Vernon had a way of motivating me every Wednesday and Sunday. This particular Sunday he said, "You are what you think you are," and even though I took it and remixed it to fit the street hustle, I walked out knowing something had to be done. I had five kids!

I had been broke for almost a year. I had reached $250,000 three or four times since I'd been released from prison and I knew I could do it again. I began making phone calls and telling my dudes that I wasn't so close to, "I got some work." My name still meant money. If I said I had dope, they would still come to buy from me. I promised robbery wasn't an option for me anymore, but I was down bad. I finally reached my dude Vel and he said that his dude wanted three bricks. I told him I had two and could get the other. I hung up and called Black…

www.ingramcontent.com/pod-product-compliance
Lightning Source LLC
Chambersburg PA
CBHW060021100426
42740CB00010B/1550